Bones in a Box:

Fear

and the

Drive for Human Control

Gary Murrell

BONES IN A BOX:

FEAR AND THE DRIVE FOR HUMAN CONTROL

Sand Wedge Publishing

Library of Congress Cataloging – in – Publication Data

Murrell, Gary

Bones in a Box: Fear and the Drive for Human Control/

Gary Murrell. – 1st ed.

Includes bibliographical (notes) reference and index

ISBN 978-1536956283

TABLE OF CONTENTS

BONES IN A BOX

INTRODUCTION

THE ENIGMA

The artist needs to understand the truth that lies at the bottom of an enigma.

-John Maeda

Hidden deep within the collective unconscious of the human psyche, buried far from conscious thought, is a powerful secret locked tightly away. It has been there always – a secret so ominous, so critical to the human condition, we expend enormous energy keeping it hidden, denying its existence. But we safeguarded the secret at a cost – an enormous cost.

I have carried this book in my head for decades. I have shared the information with friends and colleagues, and I've applied the premises of this theorem in psychotherapy work, the business world and in daily life. The veracity of this information is absolute for me; the significant challenge, however, is getting the reader past the very denial that protects him from the knowledge.

Sigmund Freud is credited with the discovery of the unconscious and with the concept of denial. While many of his theories have fallen out of favor, been regarded as fantastical, there is almost universal acceptance in the scientific community of his theory of unconscious thought and the defense mechanisms designed to keep threatening information hidden. In the Oedipus Theory, Freud suggested men, in sexual emergence, develop sexual desire for their mothers. He further posited such feelings are so repulsive, so contrary to values, the feelings and desires remain buried in the unconscious. Systems of defense are, therefore, developed to keep threatening thoughts hidden.

Nearly one hundred years after Freud's theory, brain imaging, through Positron Emission Tomography Scans, shows the area of the brain responsible for sexual love is the same area responsible for the bond between a mother and her son. There is very similar brain-blood flow and activity in the centers when mothers are bonding with children as when individuals are developing love/sexual interests in others. The Oedipal Theory, thus, has some Twenty-first Century scientific support.

Denial is the mind's way of protecting itself from the truth when information is too overwhelming to accept, or when the information does not fit into one's self-image. Upon hearing of a loved one's death you may have, at first, misinterpreted the message, because you couldn't hear it. Your brain protected you from the truth.

Several years ago I received a call. "Linda's dead." I knew who she was referring to. Linda was my wife's best friend, with whom she had grown up and lived next door for fifteen years. I asked, "What about her dad?"

"No. Linda's dead."

I responded, "I know. What about him?"

"Linda. She died."

"Linda's father died?"

There are far greater degrees of denial than occurred on that telephone call. During World War II, Hitler and the Nazis committed mass genocide of 6 million Jewish citizens, and much of the rest of the nation indicated little knowledge of the atrocities. While Jews were being loaded onto trains and delivered to death camps, the balance of the German citizenry remained relatively blind to the extermination of a people.

It has been argued the rest of Germany knew nothing of the death camps or the extent of the atrocities, but history reveals the Jews had been systematically abused for long periods of time before deportation to camps, and many Jews died of starvation and illness, as a result of the abuse, before being sent to the camps. Further, Jews who refused to get onto trains were openly shot dead in the streets. So, the argument the residents of Germany were completely unaware of the genocide is naïve. Evidence of mistreatment and murder of Jews was everywhere. All Germany knew it was unlawful to hide Jews. All Germany knew Jewish properties and businesses were being destroyed by the Nazi regime. All Germany knew Jews were being imprisoned in the ghettos of neighborhoods, unable to leave, and citizens knew Jews were being rounded up and sent to "work" camps. And from all this knowledge the veil was that Jews were being sent to work camps and treated humanely. Even if that had been the truth, where was the humanity, and why was there such global acceptance of the inhumanity?

Mass denial, social denial, is about subverting the threat of reality. The civility of a nation, or the perception of civility, maintains certain premises. A civilized nation does not murder its citizens. A civilized nation does not rape and slaughter its men, women and children. A civilized nation does not create mechanisms for mass extermination of its own people. Those are actions of an uncivilized, feral, deeply deranged nation.

The dissonance, the internal struggle, created in the minds of the average non-Jewish German was likely overwhelming. It was incomprehensible. Germany was a nation of productivity, intelligence and progression. Germany was a civilized nation. The actions of the Nazis did not fit the precept of civilization. So, it couldn't be happening. Germany could not have murdered millions of Jews. To believe otherwise would have undermined every value and belief its inhabitants held. The threat to the collective ego was too great and so, en mass, the nation of Germany denied their government was responsible for the annihilation of 6 million of its men, women and children.

Denial rises out of fear. And fear existing on a global level will bring mass denial. The human bones in a box, the hidden fear about which we, as a people, have such difficulty negotiating is such denial – a denial with enormous costs, both humanitarian and financial. It has weighed on us forever. We keep the secret from ourselves, locked tightly in a box, buried deeply from awareness. But it doesn't stay there quietly. At some level we know it's there, so we expend great effort rationalizing the seepage from our collective unconscious.

PART ONE

MAGMA

CHAPTER ONE

FEAR

Nothing in life is to be feared. It is only to be understood.

-Marie Curie

Human emotions are complex. But all emotions are based in fear. Fear is the primary emotion from which all emotions emanate. If emotions were condensed into one, the emotion would be fear, in varying degrees –intense to relatively non-existent.

Fear protects by stimulating fight or flight behavior. When fear drapes over an animal, the animal's brain immediately transitions the body, infusing chemicals that increase respiration and cardiovascular function. Senses become more acute, as the body prepares to hightail or attack.

The limbic system in the human brain is the animal brain, the brain we had before we evolved into higher level species. The limbic system produces fear, and the fear response allows us a better chance of survival in an emergency situation.

The frontal lobe is part of the more evolved brain and allows for thought, reason and planning. When the limbic system is fully engaged, the frontal lobe essentially shuts down. We don't reason; we try to survive. But often, the limbic system takes over our brains when we are not in an emergent situation – which explains road rage, screaming arguments, violence and murders resulting from poor impulse control. The limbic system is also the part of the brain used when constituents get behind boorish presidential candidates who use fear as a platform.

Using fear to plug into our undeveloped brains in not new to politics. George W. Bush used fear to control the constituency during the 911 crisis. The White House endorsed a fear response to terrorism, which sent the nation into a decade long war, caused the country to shed trillions of dollars and nearly spun the globe into financial calamity. Bill Clinton used fear as well; when his favorability ratings were diving, following accusations regarding Monica Lewinsky, President Clinton raised concerns about Iraq then ordered bombing raids on the country. His popularity soared.

Human beings are animals, and while humans are more complex than other species, it is useful to look at less developed animals to understand human functioning and how the limbic system operates. A rabbit being hunted by a coyote is in full fear response. The rabbit bolts, darting for its life. Fear is the catalyst for control and survival. The aggressor, in this case the coyote, is also being driven by fear. A coyote that does not eat will die of starvation. Behavior is always about mitigating fear.

Anxiety modulates fear. Anxiety levels determine the speed at which fear will engage. An animal more anxious or excitable will get to the fear response more quickly. This modulation of fear can be bio-chemical and inherited or conditioned, by past trauma or learned response.

Some animals will turn almost immediately to the fight mode to ward off threat - so the aggression doesn't look like fear. When dogs are snarling and gnashing teeth, we don't perceive fright. Pit-bulls raised to fight, however, are still responding to fear. Vicious attacks appear to be about anything but fear, yet it is the fear response that engages to fend off death. The same chemical response occurs in the brain of a fleeing rabbit, as in an attacking dog. The fear signal is a leap for life. The pit-bull's reaction is to attack and kill before being killed. But rabbits will bite if they are unable to escape, and dogs will run if it is deemed the more likely avenue for survival.

Anger and rage also come from fear. Both are reactions to threat. Many models of emotion run horizontally or in a scatter-gram. I submit the model of emotion runs vertically. Fear is at the base and love and all the emotions in between are, at varying degrees, reduced levels of fear. Love is feeling safe, cared for and in a predictably threat-free place. Love does not occur without sense of safety and trust. One cannot enjoy love and happiness while under attack. Only when fear dissipates are love and joy possible.

ALTRUISM *

↑

LOVE

↑

HAPPINESS

↑

JOY

↑

CURIOUSITY

↑

REMORSE

↑

SADNESS

↑

ANGER

↑

RAGE

DISGUST→ ↑ ←JEALOUSY

FEAR

UNCONSCIOUS ↓ ———————————— CONSCIOUS ↑

FEAR (OF DEATH)

↑↑↑↑↑

↑UNCONSCIOUS↑

Consider the diagram above when trying to make sense of Andy Brach's assault and murder of his wife in 1974. Andy's life had not been the best. While his intellect was probably in the average to low average range, his verbal skills were below average, so he didn't process information well through language. His skill set was as a handyman with strong visual/spatial applications. So, when he learned his wife was seeing another man and planning to leave him, Andy's fear surged. He had never had a lot in life and didn't see things changing. He and his wife had been married eleven years, and there were no children. His job didn't offer much promise. His marriage was how he defined himself, in large part, and he saw that segment of his life dying. The significant, impending loss lit up his fear center, hardwired to the unconscious terror of death. Andy's higher brain shut down and his limbic system, the part of his brain wired for survival, took over. Andy's system kicked into a course of mitigating the fear and threat – it miscued fear as threat of death – and into one of survival and control. His language area, not a strength in the best of situations, shut down. (The adage, "rendered speechless," likely has its basis in this phenomenon.) When Andy came home early from work, he did not find his wife with her lover, as he had half expected, but he did find two wine glasses on the bedside table, the bottle empty. Andy was never aware of the fear. He had no conscious clue his system had gone into control mode – survival mode. He only felt rage. He found his wife in the bathtub, two candles burning on the edge of the porcelain white. When she told him to get out, that it was over between them, Andy's rage, rooted in fear of loss, threw him into an animalistic fury of control. He strangled her and held her under water until the threat was extinguished. Her death was ruled homicide by asphyxiation. Andy spent the next eight years in a penitentiary.

Brain studies show that oxytocin, the chemical responsible for providing sense of elation connected with love, suppresses activity in the fear centers in the brain. So physiologically, love cannot exist when fear levels are high. The two emotions do not function simultaneously; love is literally dependent on suppression or absence of fear. Hugging and kissing release a flood of oxytocin. The hormone is highly addictive, and street drugs that replicate the results of oxytocin can be very habit forming.

Trust is a seal of approval, a tag certifying the fear center need not be engaged. Trust allows love to take hold. Love cannot take shape where trust does not exist. Trust is the bridge between abating fear and allowing love. So, fear is shut off when trust is engaged. Oxytocin, not surprisingly, has been dubbed the "trust drug," because the release of oxytocin promotes trust by mitigating fear. As levels of trust increase, capacity for love increases; likewise, when trust levels dissipate, so does capacity for love. When trust is breached, fear intensifies, because trust is more intellectual, and fear will wash it out like a flooding, raging river.

It is very important to understand fear as the base emotion for all emotions. Fear is the emotional door between the conscious and unconscious worlds. Sometimes we are aware of our fears. Sometimes fear remains hidden. As fear is the gateway to all other emotions, it is fear that drives nearly all decisions. We are in denial about most fear, because it sits below conscious levels. Our deepest fear, the fear hidden well beneath the depths of our unconscious, is the fear of death. Thus, it is the fear of death, ultimately, that drives all emotions and all actions.

While, intellectually, we acknowledge death is imminent, we are in emotional denial we will die. We have conversations about death, but those are on an intellectual and not emotional level. When we truly look death in the face, when our path brings us to the edge of a precarious, loosely footed thousand foot cliff, we spin into panic and terror. The protective shield of denial is torn away, and the suppressed, unconscious fear emerges and squeezes into consciousness.

Death is the ultimate loss of control, and so, in our elaborate symphony of denial, we project control; when we feel the emergence of fear (potential death) we project control (life). Complete loss of control is death, so our collective denial takes the form of control. The illusion of control allows us to deny mortality and suppress fear. And as a society, we spend billions of dollars and sacrifice millions of lives to buoy the illusion of control. The constant wrestling with suppression of fear and the illusion of control are the Bones in a Box; it is this ubiquitous force that drives most of our lives.

**Altruism, a state of selfless giving, is a counter-intuitive concept; those who engage in altruism are performing good deeds because they are reinforced at some level, be it feeling good about oneself or expectation of rewards in the afterlife. It is, therefore, arguably not selfless but self-gratifying.*

The Raven - by Edgar Allan Poe (excerpt)

Once upon a midnight dreary, while I pondered, weak and weary,
Over many a quaint and curious volume of forgotten lore,
While I nodded, nearly napping, suddenly there came a tapping,
As of some one gently rapping, rapping at my chamber door.
''Tis some visitor,' I muttered, 'tapping at my chamber door-
Only this, and nothing more.'

And the silken sad uncertain rustling of each purple curtain
Thrilled me- filled me with fantastic terrors never felt before;
So that now, to still the beating of my heart, I stood repeating,
''Tis some visitor entreating entrance at my chamber door-
Some late visitor entreating entrance at my chamber door;-
This it is, and nothing more.'

Deep into that darkness peering, long I stood there wondering,
fearing,
Doubting, dreaming dreams no mortals ever dared to dream before;
But the silence was unbroken, and the stillness gave no token,
And the only word there spoken was the whispered word, 'Lenore!'
This I whispered, and an echo murmured back the word, 'Lenore!'-
Merely this, and nothing more.

And the Raven, never flitting, still is sitting, still is sitting

On the pallid bust of Pallas just above my chamber door;
And his eyes have all the seeming of a demon's that is dreaming,
And the lamplight o'er him streaming throws his shadow on the floor;
And my soul from out that shadow that lies floating on the floor
Shall be lifted- nevermore.

CHAPTER TWO

FEAR IS DEATH IS FEAR

The basis of optimism is sheer terror.

-Oscar Wilde

Drilling down a bit, all fear is about loss. The ultimate fear, the panic all fear is sitting upon, is death. Death represents ultimate loss of control. So, all fear is about losing control. This is the most important concept of this book – all emotion is based in fear and all fear is based in the terror of losing control, the ultimate loss of control being death; and taking control, or erecting an illusion of control, mitigates fear.

Every emotion can find its way back to fear of death, and, conversely, much of human life is about compensating and over-reacting to that fear – through control.

Most individuals do not obsess about death. The fact people don't typically obsess is clear indication a comprehensive system of denial exists. Intellectually, we know we are going to die, but most of us do not perseverate on the reality; we use denial to protect ourselves, and we overcompensate with fantasies of immortality. It is the way we cope; we are in denial about death, because it is too emotionally threatening to deal with on a daily basis.

So, if denial is an understandable way to deal with the fear of death, why write about it? Why not just leave it hidden? We don't leave information hidden, because it is our nature to better understand ourselves and our world. Psychotherapy is an exercise in self understanding, unveiling of truth, bringing to consciousness issues and concerns buried in denial and self-deception. A problem buried will always make its way to the surface, though it may be cloaked. When we construct alter-realities, in order to maintain denial, the truth pokes the surface and blossoms into symptoms of psychopathology.

Several years ago I treated a woman who had paralysis of her left arm. She had been referred to me by physicians who could find nothing physically wrong. Her arm had been essentially non-functioning for two years. When I inquired about details of her life at the time of onset of the paralysis, she was vague and said it was a long time ago. I was not concerned, however, about her memory for facts, as the real issue, if it was indeed psychological, was buried in her subconscious. We peeled away the layers, danced around innocuous items, then landed on an argument that had occurred between her husband and the patient at about the time she lost functioning of her left arm. This was not a typical argument for them. The patient's husband was very large and imposing, and in this one instance, she stated, he grabbed hold of her upper arm and pushed her into the refrigerator. Her recollection brought a great deal of emotion, a strong fear response, and she openly cried. I asked her to another session, this time inviting her husband. I broached the subject of the argument two years before, and her husband acknowledged the argument but minimized the significance. The patient became angry at his downplaying the physicality of the confrontation, and while her husband attempted to quash her responses, she was invited by me to talk about how she felt, about the level of threat she believed she had endured and the anger and lack of control she had felt over her situation. Her anger was a good sign, because it evidenced her shift from victim to going on the offensive, an attempt to take control back. After her very emotional outpouring, her husband acknowledged her feelings and apologized. We scheduled another session, and upon their arrival the patient reported she was feeling well. Additionally, the problem she had been having with her arm had spontaneously abated. She was reticent to connect it to the last session, but she did not believe we needed to meet again.

Conversion Disorder is a somatic symptom disorder that has no apparent physical cause. In this case, the patient felt threatened and powerless by her husband's assault, and her unconscious fear over his behavior manifested in a physical disability – a loss of physical control. Bringing the issues to light, transferring from the unconscious to the conscious her fear and anger, and feeling heard by her husband resulted in restoration of her abilities.

An issue cannot be fixed if there is no awareness a problem exists. Bringing issues to light allows us to determine whether or not there are problems with the way we are functioning below the surface. Mass denial about death certainly costs society significantly, both mentally and fiscally.

We deny mortality, because the information is overwhelming to our sense of self. Individuals talk openly about death, but they do so with emotional disengagement. It is an intellectual exercise. Death becomes academic, theoretical, but the emotional detachment surrounding mortality is really an unreasonable reaction to the proposition of death. The detachment is a symptom of denial.

Denial is eroded when we experience near death. Post-Traumatic Stress Disorder is a common side effect of having faced a near-death event. Denial thins out, and individuals who have faced war, police action or victimization are far more prone to panic and anxiety. The denial stops working so well.

When death comes close, the fear is un-caged. Regardless of how prepared you are, death is an unknown. It is the antithesis of life. We can talk about pain, but if we aren't feeling it at the moment, it is only academic. Death is the same.

When we edge closer to death, fear warns us. When fear increases, we seek control. Control is life. Loss of control is death. All animals vie for control. And when humans cannot control they project fantasy of control. As long as we believe we are in control, we are not dying.

In the next several chapters, I will reveal the enormous construct associated with our delusion of control. Physically, it is everywhere, and its ubiquity leaks into every crevice of humanity.

The Tree

The forest. Sunlight angling in, lighting the foliage. In the mist of the morning, a great oak rises, spreading its limbs widely. Other trees are dwarfed, giving way. The great oak has claimed the area, the sunlight, the dew and air. Leaves rattle in the breeze, audible, speaking the names of the limbs, the insects, the years. Two hundred feet tall. As much wide. Traversing down the bark, the thick trunk. Down to the soil. Its roots running along the earth's surface, spreading out like a pod into the loam. The tree dives beneath the soil. Runs hundreds of feet deep. Holds the earth and drinks the world. As much beneath the surface as above. But we cannot see; we are oblivious to the oak beneath the surface. We are aware of the root, the bugs, the soil, the earth. But consciously we register what we see. We have lost our spiritual acuity, the knowledge of things not seen, of realities not in our faces. So much occurs beneath the surface. Buried. It is no less there, however. All that is apparent and all that is unseen makes up the totality.

PART TWO

ERUPTION

CHAPTER THREE

CONTROL

You must learn to let go. Release the stress. You were never in control anyway.

-Steve Maraboli

In November 2014, Nik Wallenda, of the Flying Wallendas, walked a high wire rope, without a safety net, between two skyscrapers in Chicago. The winds gusted to 30 mph. The wire was stretched at a 19 degree angle, an incline that would seem fairly steep if you were out for a walk in tennis shoes. The cord was suspended more than 60 stories above earth, and Mr. Wallenda performed the act blindfolded.

What would possess a man to do such a thing? Did he have a death wish? Was he tempting fate? To the contrary – he was mitigating fear by exhibiting control. Thousands watched, because they needed to vicariously experience the control, as well.

Those with greatest fear of losing control exhibit the greatest levels of controlling behavior. Control is compensation for fear; the greater the fear, the greater the need to control. Control is a drive to live, to take action. The act of controlling reduces fear and provides the cloak of denial that we are mortal and vulnerable.

While this likely sounds gloomy and dire, it really isn't so bad. Reality has not changed, just because we are facing the truth. And there is a pure benefit to having knowledge. Much of that will be broached in the final section of the book, but knowledge of denial is the beginning of enlightenment and health – as was for the patient with the paralyzed arm.

While compensation for fear of loss of control is to control, over-compensation can be catastrophic. We talk of the "Napoleonic Complex" when describing a ranting, micromanaging boss, but consider there really was a Napoleon. A Mussolini. A Hitler.

Many recent studies on the effects of narcissistic CEOs in business demonstrate the dangers of over-control. Narcissistic personalities are, by definition, grandiose, starved for admiration and lacking empathy. Narcissists demand respect, whether or not they have earned it, and have fantasies about unlimited success and power. They believe they are uniquely superior and should only associate with others who are highly successful. They exploit others, tend to be arrogant and have deep sense of entitlement. All these features are compensations for an underlying fragile ego. At an unconscious level, individuals with narcissistic personality are self-doubting and believe they have no control. Internal weakness results in efforts of compensation for fears of being out of control - by over-controlling. They project grand importance, because they fear they are small and insignificant. They have fantasies about unlimited success, because they fear they are failures.

In order to fuel the delusion of superiority, narcissists demand unwarranted respect, spend a great deal of others' money on themselves, surround themselves with successful people and fire people who question their authority and supremacy. Their exercise in control, through employment terminations, business acquisitions and company change demonstrates their power and feeds the delusion they are, indeed, in control. The underlying fear is still death; and the resulting projection of control screams life and quiets the fear. Change always demonstrates power, because only those in charge can effect top down change.

* * *

The easiest route to change is destruction, an assertion of omnipotence, as with children who step on or crush ants with sticks. Narcissistic CEOs tend to destroy businesses and drive profits into the basement. Merrill Lynch, Leyman Brothers, Goldman's, Google and Amazon are all companies having had narcissistic CEOs who squandered millions of dollars in attempts to elevate their self-images (yachts, hundreds of millions of dollars for beach houses, and one $42 million perpetual clock).

Tucker Vale took the position of CEO at a mid-sized textile company in 2003. He had a fair amount of mid-management experience, but the position of CEO was a gargantuan step. He came without executive management experience, but Vale had a narcissistic personality, so he believed he was due the position, and he was able to convince the Board of Directors he was the right person for the job.

While Vale was an imposing man, who spoke quickly and with command, at his core he had great doubt in his abilities. So, Vale overcompensated. He feared he didn't have control, so he over-controlled. In his first six months on the job, Vale fired six of his first line managers, costing the company 120 years of experience. His conversations with other managers and staff were littered with suggestions of employment termination, a semi-veiled threat affirming he was in charge.

Vale demanded allegiance, though he did little to garner the respect and trust of those who were supposed to be following him. He did little to support his employees from the top. After only eight months in his position as CEO, Vale convinced the Board of Directors to change the shipping company responsible for delivering textiles from Asia. He sold the Board on the reduced cost and the promise to deliver goods 15% more quickly. Vale's management team was opposed. The textile company had been using the same shipping business for 28 years, and there were strong relationships and a proven record. Vale moved quickly, ignoring concerns of his remaining managers, and the transition occurred. Nobody dared go over Vale and to the Board. They had seen what had happened to six other managers.

The move was disastrous. Late shipments resulted in erosion of trust that had been built over decades. Two major accounts terminated, and the textile company Vale took over nearly went under.

Vale's actions had devastating consequences for those around him. His need to control was borne out of fear of not having control. His fear of failure drove his need to demonstrate his control. He fired people, because that is an unquestionable action of control. He made significant and reckless change in the company, because dramatic change suggests control.

A direct relationship exists between Perceived Threat and Response Control Reaction. The greater the perceived threat of losing control, the greater the response to regaining control. What may be perceived as a threat to one person, however, may not be threatening to another. Further, perception of threat of loss of control is predicated on experiences. A person who had a relatively uneventful childhood is not going to perceive threat of loss of control the same as a person whose father or mother psychologically and physically abused him.

The lower the perceived threat, physically or emotionally, the lower the risk of a Control Reaction. Remember, the need to control is always based in fear. While all fear is not directly about death, the roots are always grounded in fear of death. The response is to move away from the potential of death. Calm begets calm. Absolute threat of violence triggers response to control, up through and including homicide/suicide.

The Vale vignette exemplifies how over-control, compensatory control, can be destructive. But Vale's cost was to one company. Compensatory control can be so much more destructive, and at such greater cost.

Kim Jong-un, of North Korea, exemplifies a narcissistic supreme leader, whose immature gestures of control manifest in brutal executions, demands of loyalty and admiration from all and threats of murder and nuclear war as means of exhibiting control. Kim Jong-un screams unconscious fear of losing control through exhibition of over-control and oppression.

Control is ubiquitous. There is nothing that does not have the fingerprint of control on it. It is apparent in our sexual proclivities, our architecture and the multi-billion dollar industries of sports and media. It results in homicide, suicide, terrorism and war. The need to control is fundamental, thus the need to understand control is critical to our human existence.

ACTING OUT

Poking a stick at the hill of ants,

New Baby Brother came home,

It was all so cool – before,

New baby brother came home,

Cooing. Crying.

"Be a nice big brother" – sing-song – "be nice to him,"

Army of ants, all in their place,

Lugging bits of sand. Fall in line.

A busted tree limb, poking the mound,

Kill those shits

Smash those domes.

Mash your brains,

I'm in control.

CHAPTER FOUR

SUBLIMATION

I'm sorry. I use my rapier wit to hide my inner pain.

-Cassandra Clare

As noted earlier, defense mechanisms are the brain's way of protecting from harmful reality. Sublimation is a defense mechanism by which we manage to transfer our emotions into constructive, rather than destructive, activities. An individual with physically aggressive desires may channel that energy into work as a surgeon. An artist may write about murder or paint macabre scenes. Freud believed sublimation was the most mature defense mechanism.

Jack Kervorkian became known in the 1990's as "Dr. Death," yet emanation of the ideas and behaviors that made him famous in the 1990's were germinating in Kervorkian for decades. Kervorkian received his medical degree from the University of Michigan in 1952. As a medical school resident, he proposed allowing death row prisoners options of death by anesthesia, so bodies could be preserved for experimentation and organs harvested.

His fascination led him to specialize in pathology. After working with dead bodies for twenty-five years, he retired from medicine, moved to Long Beach, California and tried a career in writing and the fine arts. His drawings and paintings mostly depicted skulls and death. In the 1980's, Kervorkian again pursued the idea of anesthetizing prisoners to death, but this time he caught the attention of the California legislature, which began studies of the idea. He visited the Netherlands in 1987 to study the Dutch method for assisted suicide then moved back to Detroit, where he began taking out newspaper advertisements publicizing his interest in assisted suicide for the terminally and chronically ill. In 1990, Dr. Kervorkian successfully helped a woman diagnosed with Alzheimer's Disease end her life.

Kervorkian followed the suicide in Detroit with a string of 130 more assisted terminations of life. As his activities and cause gained more publicity, he received more push-back from prosecutors. He was charged and acquitted three times. Finally, Kervorkian went beyond assisting with suicide and actually injected a patient with a life-ending serum. He videotaped the session and sent it to the news show "60 Minutes." The tape led to his conviction, after which he spent 8 years in prison for second degree murder. Kervorkian died in 2011 at the age of 83.

Kervorkian is an interesting study in sublimation. While Kervorkian's objective in legalizing assisted suicide may be admirable and ethically arguable, the underlying motivation was not endearing. His fervor for studying and witnessing death was driven by unconscious desires, by his own need to control; and he found an avenue for legitimizing his macabre need to kill and watch people die. But most cases of sublimation do not cross the line, wherein defenses break down, and the sublimation succumbs to bald, unconscious desires. Kervorkian provides a continuum of the mind defended through high level sublimation and breakdown of the defenses.

Neurosurgeon and recent presidential candidate Ben Carson provides a more successful application of sublimation. Carson grew up poor on the streets of Detroit. As an early teen, he reports, he began to get into trouble and, at one point, pulled a knife on another young man. His mother, who was essentially unable to read, remanded Carson to reading and providing her with book reports. Carson later became a leading pediatric neurosurgeon, converting his use of a blade for illicit purposes to a virtuoso's adept handling of a scalpel.

Carson went on to become the Chief Pediatric Neurosurgeon at Johns Hopkins Hospital.

Sublimation is an outlet for suppressed, unconscious drives. If fear of death is imminent, and if that fear is suppressed through activities of control, evidence of sublimation of the drive to control would be abundant. And it is. It is revealed in sports, movies, government and war. The sublimation of control, or the need to perpetuate the illusion of control, is virtually everywhere.

DOWN GOES FRAZIER

Joe Frazier. George Foreman. Frazier had just upended the Great Mohammed Ali whose record was 56 wins, 5 losses.

Frazier had taken the World Heavy Weight Title from the reigning champ, Mohammed Ali.

Foreman was scared. Knees shaking.

And then - one minute, thirty-five seconds into the second round:

"Down goes Frazier!

Down goes Frazier!

Down goes Frazier!

He is as poised as can be!" - Howard Coselle

GEORGE FOREMAN DESTROYS JOE FRAZIER!

CHAPTER FIVE

SPORTS

What makes something special is not just what you have to gain, but what you feel there is to lose.

-Andre Agassi

Professional sports is a nearly $500 billion annual industry in the United States. That averages nearly $2,500 every year for every individual over 18 years. The global sports industry comes in at about $1.5 trillion. Where we invest our money and where we spend our time is indicative of priority we place on interests and commodities. Professional sports are, inarguably, extremely important.

Many radio stations focus exclusively on sports. Entire sections of nearly every newspaper in America are dedicated to sports. Yet, there aren't daily newspaper sections on politics, or legislation or humanitarian measures. Why?

You could argue we played sports as youngsters and want to relive the competitive verve. But we all went to school and had some good times; nobody is advocating for spectator schools. The reason professional sports are so important is they represent a collective, societal sublimation of our need to control. At its most superficial level, sporting activities parallel warlike conflict and opposition. But at the deepest level, sports are about control and about spectators vicariously realizing control through the actions of others.

Sports are society's projection of unconscious need to be in control, and sports provide the illusion of control. Sports are overcompensation for feeling lack of control. The sports industry in the United States equates to the approximate gross domestic product (GDP) of Norway; the global sports industry exceeds the GDP of the United States – this so the impossible can be imagined, the uncontrollable controlled. Through the sporting venue, we successfully fool ourselves into thinking we have control, and the feeling of control dissipates our fear.

Professional pitchers throw baseballs at a hundred miles per hour, and if that isn't enough, the ball breaks at the last fraction of a second or drops off, and the batter, having less than a second to make a decision, swings a slim piece of wood to try to hit the small sphere where nobody happens to be. Defensive plays are awe inspiring, outfielders sprinting backwards and snatching balls in basket catches or diving, outstretched, to haul balls in. To make control even more elusive, sports are played on ice and on horseback, in the rain and in snow. When the feat of control is accomplished, we feel great. All sporting events are played with likelihood of control against the odds.

A six foot, seven inch player in the NBA is not so odd. When you see an individual in the grocery store that size you think superhuman. On the court or the gridiron, these gargantuan men hit one another, while attempting to maintain control of balls or pucks that will go any which way when striking a surface. Every week we live for this control. If you truly enjoy sports, you know the players. They become family. And when they control something not controllable, you own it, because they are part of you.

And there aren't just the games. There are pre-games and post-games, where we see the highlights, the phenomenal catches and the powerful hits. Replays highlight the impossible catches, tight ends leaping over the backs of tackles, diving snags, golf swings that crush balls from tall saw-grass and seat them gently next to the pin. We devour the plays, because it confirms we are superhuman. Immortal. We are in control, and therefore our denial of death is, for that moment, rationalized.

In the United States a professional starting football quarterback, a man whom we might say has no direct bearing on our (conscious) lives, is paid an annual salary exceeding 43 times the salary of the U.S. President (arguably the most powerful position on Earth). It seems nonsensical, unless you attribute the value for the right reasons –we are paying for the illusion of control. The football quarterback provides sublimated need.

Intellectually, we recognize the $20,000,000 salary for a baseball player is absurd. We argue that sports is entertainment, and that is true; but why do we compensate entertainers so well? Why does a man who contributes relatively little intellectually - who does not problem solve ecological, humanitarian, philosophical or medical conundrums – become the bearer of great world treasures? His rewards are bestowed by a society indebted to his gift of control, his projection we are immortal.

Sports allay our fears of losing control by controlling all, for a time. And it is not a small contribution. Our need to mitigate fear through control is so pervasive, so substantial, we pay a price we consider to be insane. Yet, in pubs and living rooms across the globe, fans jump and scream, moan and curse. The energy and explosion of emotion is common; but what truly explains it? The greater the emotional charge, the more explosive the reaction. We don't just want our teams to win, we need them to prevail. Fans sometimes drop into days of depression following a major loss, and in cities around the world, cars are overturned and set fire at the climax of a season. The emotions stem from fear, and fear results in need for control.

One of the most popular and controversial legends in baseball history occurred during the 1932 World Series games, in which Babe Ruth purportedly pointed to the center field seats – calling his home run. With two strikes on him, Ruth stepped out of the batters' box, raised his right arm and signaled with two fingers toward the flag in center field. The next pitch Ruth drilled into the center field seats. Whether or not his gesture was predictive or not, the sensation, which still lives today - more than eighty years later - is testament to our obsession with the power and control we receive from sporting events. It was not only the towering home run, from perhaps the best player ever to grace the field, but Ruth's prediction that underscored the control. Predictability is a factor of control on its own, and Ruth's blast into deep center after calling the shot, sets any sports fan on fire. We feel empowered, bound by no limits, for a moment in time invincible and immortal. Fear is driven down because we are filled with vicarious control.

ONE

You bend my mind

Curl inside my brain

Constant

Senses crackling – static

Lips and mouth

Hungry, eager, wet

A lily splayed

Enigmatic beauty, esoteric form, beguiling aroma

Open

Rising

Consuming, infusing

One in the dark universe. A soul. Together. Forever.

CHAPTER SIX

SEX

Everything in the world is about sex except sex. Sex is about power.

-Oscar Wilde

Sex is everywhere, and despite the privacy which we, on a nearly global level, desire when involved in sex, sex squeezes out and permeates culture at all levels. Sex is woven into advertising, movies and novels and it dances on the fringe of non-sexual relationships. Internet searches for erotic content make up an estimated 13% of all queries. While we try as a society to control sex, to repress sex, it will not be contained.

The act of sex is physical, but much about sex operates below the surface, at the unconscious level. Sex is a drive, as is the need for sustenance and the need to control. Because we defend against many of our sexual urges, we hide a great deal of our sexuality from ourselves. Individuals reared in particularly chaste environments, due to parents' histories or religious proclivities, may avoid even the most casual contact with the opposite sex, including hand shaking, dancing and proximity. While the animal brain in all of us is seeking sexual union, the superego is hiding the desire and throwing up defensive strategies. Thus, a woman's sexual urges may be hidden beneath drab clothing and overly prudish interactions with men.

Much of what occurs in the bedroom (or on the kitchen counter) is representative of what is going on in a relationship. A great deal about a relationship can be gleaned from the sexuality, just as much can be interpreted about an individual's deeper thoughts and emotions through dream analysis. When tension, anger, insecurity and lack of trust are present in a relationship, it will show up in the sex in the relationship.

Freud theorized there were three parts to the psyche – the id, the ego and the superego. The ego is that image the person considers herself to be. The superego is the parent in the psyche, the moral and ethical compass, the conscience. The id is the unconscious part of the psyche that is not tempered - the wild child. From a Freudian perspective, sex operates from the id but is suppressed by the superego.

The id gives into salacious desires and dark needs. Yet, realizing those desires may be very threatening to one's idealized self-image, the psyche denies the desires exist. The id and the superego are at odds, fighting out what is consciously presented to the ego. So, the darkest desires hiding in the subconscious may never work themselves into the consciousness of an individual. The desire will still be there, and the individual's actions and slipped comments may provide clues, but the door will remain closed.

Sexual fantasies provide windows to repressed thoughts. Fantasies, which may reveal unabashed notions of sex, are sometimes disturbing and seemingly out of character. Rather than locking up and attempting to squeeze the thoughts out, let them in, look at them in undefended ways and wonder what they mean. Having a fantasy doesn't necessarily mean you intend or wish to act on the thoughts. There isn't any more risk of falling into debauchery because of sexual fantasy than murdering your neighbor because you enjoy murder mysteries. Just look and wonder.

Fantasies in and of themselves are not bad. They just are. When fantasies become threatening to the ego, many defend against them, denying and repressing. Looking at sexual fantasies and wondering about them, however, provides insight into our makeup and our deeper drives.

In "I and Thou," Martin Buber notes, "the themes of sexual fantasies are remarkably consistent worldwide and reveal more about innate tendencies than cultural norms." Buber is speaking of the underlying sexual drive and how acculturation runs contrary to social expectations. He continues, "Most (fantasies) are deviant to cultural norms. Implicit and explicit societal rules are often the enemy of sex and use stories and rules to suppress sexual expressions, enforce taboos and conceal deviant sexual interests."

These are not social or cultural expressions, but rather a collective expression of the unconscious. Sexual fantasies go beyond the act of sex. Because they sit in the unconscious and spill into our consciousness, they carry our strongest desires and our deepest hidden fears. If sexual fantasies were simply about sex and orgasm there would be no revelation of emotion with the fantasies.

Not surprisingly, fantasies seep through the unconscious, dripping evidence of our struggles with control. Unconscious thought is always banging on the door of consciousness, and the hidden fears and anxieties regarding control jump the train of sexual fantasy and transport the emotions from unconscious to conscious levels.

Sexual fantasy is evidence of the control drive. The rape fantasy does not suggest an individual wants to be raped; it is a fantasy about relinquishing control. The fantasy serves two interrelated purposes. The first is to satisfy the desire to have abandoned sex. In fantasy, rape absolves responsibility for having sex, since it is forced. Secondly, and more significant to the subject matter, the rape fantasy is about control and losing control.

While the underlying drive is to maintain control at all times, there is the complicating fantasy of not having to be in control. Being in control all the time is wearing, exhausting, and so we fantasize about being taken, ravished and ignored in terms of our real wants and desires; ultimately, our desire is to be taken care of, to relax and not worry about having to control our worlds.

Bondage fantasies and the world of sado-masochistic desires are closely related to rape fantasies; the control aspect is obvious. Despite the fantasy of being controlled, however, the individual having the fantasy is really in control. She is confident nothing will go wrong. In acting out bondage fantasies, a partner is rendered completely out of control. Sex occurs at the will of the free partner. Or it would seem. The reality is that with consensual bondage, there is typically significant trust and a designated safe word which, when given, releases the bonds. The person bound is really in control of being out of control. So, trust allows a partner to experience the feeling of being out of control, while ultimately being in control. Being in control of being out of control is akin to feelings evoked watching horror films (the viewer is in a safe setting, while facing the ultimate fear of being completely out of control). The next chapter will discuss how movies sublimate our need for control.

Freud discussed a notion called Theory of Recapitulation, a hypothesis first popularized by Ernst Haeckel and hemmed to Darwin's Theory of Evolution. The Theory of Recapitulation (ontogeny recapitulates phylogeny) suggests embryos go through all the evolutionary stages of the species in the womb. Freud expanded this to a psychological level, essentially stating people put themselves into negative situations over and over to attempt to master outcomes. He posited girls abused by fathers, for instance, continue to put themselves back into similar situations with abusive adult men in an attempt to get it right. Girls put themselves back into those situations not because they believe they deserve to be treated badly, but because they are attempting to gain control of their lives and cannot accept they are not in control. The fear of facing an abusive situation is not as frightening as not having control.

In the book, "My Secret Garden," a compilation of sexual fantasies by Nancy Friday, an anonymous woman describes her true account of having been kidnapped, repeatedly raped and held captive by three men for two days. She believed if she cooperated she would not be physically harmed, so she acquiesced. At some point, she actively decided to slip into a subservient role. Near the end of her captivity she was threatened with harm if she did engage in a final submission, and in the minutes that followed, the writer described images and concepts which would forever be burned into her memory. Her captor represented all control - he symbolized control. In the end, she described feeling victorious; she believed she had attained ultimate control, and she felt powerful. She had been immersed in fear, with no control; she then took ultimate control and emerged from the fear. She was released soon after, but she left believing her sexual mastery saved her life. Later, she married a man, and she reported living a submissive life, reliving her ordeal, ultimately mitigating fear through sexual control.

As with subservience, humiliation fantasies are based in losing control. Relinquishing control. The fantasy may be about being exposed to others or about being forced to do something submissive or subjugating. Humiliation is public embarrassment of being found out of control. The fantasy is still encoded; it does not appear on the surface to be about facing fear of loss of control. The conscious brain is focused on sexual humiliation. There is no conscious focus on fear or control. In the end though, pressure building from the repressed fear is abated by facing the fear through fantasy.

Cross-dressing is giving control away. A high powered attorney, who must show aggression in the court room and must control an opposing attorney, may perceive, based on memories of his mother or grandmother, the female gender does not need to be in control. Thus, he takes on a more submissive gender role and assumes the physical form. For such individuals control can be a burden and cross-dressing, for a few, provides relief. The risk of being found out makes him feel vulnerable – juxtaposition of the aggressive role he may otherwise play in life.

Domination fantasies, on the other hand, are overtly about control. In playing out such fantasies, the dominant needs a submissive partner. Typically, domination and submissive fantasies are reciprocal; there are empathetic role reversals. Domination and submission fantasies hide less the unconscious encoding of having complete control and complete loss of control. The fantasies act as a pressure valve, releasing pent up repression of fears of losing control and pressures of having to maintain control.

The categories of sexual fantasies are many and varied. They include vampires, which are innately immortal; zombies, which defy death but can be slaughtered without remorse; urination fantasies, or humiliating loss of control; diaper wearing and infantilism; vomiting; exhibitionism; voyeurism and on and on. Consider a sexual category of fantasy, and it inarguably represents control and loss of control.

During sexual orgasm we lose emotional and physical control. The muscles involuntarily spasm, we may yell out or clench and afterward, during the refractory phase, relax. During orgasm, the fear center of the brain is repressed. Orgasms occur when we feel safe, when it is safe to let go and not manage control. The sensation derived from orgasm – letting go, falling out of control and slipping into a stage of relaxation – is something all individuals seek. We feel the need to be in control, but we really want to relax, let go and feel safe.

Sex and control are both drives, the foundations of which reside in the unconscious. Both sex and control emerge from the unconscious in disguise. Some sexual desires are repressed and some ideation is encoded, so it fits with the ego's sense of self. Often, the sexuality and control drives emerged entangled, with sexual fantasy being wrapped in symbolic expressions of control and loss of control.

POPCORN

The buttery, burnt smell of the movie theater wraps around you. You settle in, surround-sound vibrating your bones, taking you out of your world and placing you in another.

You're annoyed by a whisper or the interruption of a cell phone, because you want to assimilate to the land or the room or the time of the movie as closely as possible. You want to get to know the characters and step into the protagonist's role, become him or her, for a couple hours.

You are elsewhere. You may face villains, but you will be out of harm's way. You may feel the humiliation of social faux pas, without wearing the embarrassment into next week. You might feel strong, sexy and invincible. Alive. But it's all a safe, harmless, vicarious experience.

Settle back. Leave your vulnerabilities behind for a time. Let Hollywood send you into another universe. And enjoy the popcorn.

CHAPTER SEVEN

MOVIES AND SUCH

As far as I'm concerned, men like you were put on this world to entertain women like me.

-Susan Elizabeth Phillips

The 007 movie series, based on Ian Flemming's novels, has produced over twenty James Bond films since 1962. Even if you're not a fan, the fact a movie series has lasted, and has created box office hits for over 50 years, is impressive. The series has grossed over 6 billion dollars since its debut film, "Dr. No." Bond, an English spy, suppresses evil (death), survives outrageous attacks and maintains an easy, always in control demeanor. He is cool, unfettered, and he always gets the girl. It is important that, from the beginning of each movie, we know he will live, because immortality is at the heart of Bond.

J.K. Rowlings' Harry Potter series is the highest grossing film series in the world, reaping $7.7 billion in box office receipts. Again, the protagonists deal with evil but have been given magical powers to maintain control and ward off death. The lead, Harry Potter, is an unlikely hero, growing up in a home in which he is bullied and mistreated. It is clearly established that Harry is a victim of his childhood world. He then enters into a subliminal place of witchery and magic, and Harry gains all the tools necessary to control his world and defeat death.

Neither James Bond nor Harry Potter feed our rational, conscious minds. But it isn't about the rational; it's about the unconscious need for all of us to feel in control. For a couple hours, we are fueled by vicarious feelings of having complete command. From an intellectual perspective, the movies are nonsensical. The characters survive situations that would result in certain death for any mortal. So, what gratification do movie-goers receive that compels them to shell out billions of dollars for irrational, unrealistic experiences? The gratification is feeling in control.

If an underlying, unconscious propensity to be in control does not exist, why is Hollywood a multi-billion dollar industry? Why are the majority of blockbuster films action movies, with leading men and women with uncanny control of their worlds blowing things up? And what is rational about adults flocking to theaters to watch superheroes in tights and capes using special powers to control and eliminate evil?

Raimi's trilogy Spiderman movies have grossed a combined $2.5 billion, and the six Spiderman movies dating back to 2004 have grossed $3.7 billion, placing the series at sixth in all time box office sales. The Batman movies series has pulled in nearly $2.5 billion. Citizen Kane, by comparison, which many critics believe to be the greatest film ever made, grossed $1.5 million, which equates to about $12.5 million in 1989 dollars. The first Batman movie, in 1989, grossed $40,500,000 – in its first weekend.

In the horror genre, protagonists are threatened with messy deaths. Horror movies are generally graphic and bloody, bringing to greater consciousness fear of death and mortality. Viewers are experiencing base fear, rather than the more insulated fear delivered in science fiction, animation and superhero movies.

There have been nine "Nightmare on Elm Street" movies. The series has spanned 25 years and grossed nearly $450 million. Our rational and conscious sides make fun of the films, but millions have purchased tickets to be frightened out of their pants. Why - if we want control, would we pay to experience being out of control? Because we want to believe when we feel out of control we really are in control. We want mastery over our fear.

When Freddie Kruger goes after a scantily clad teen, viewers yell, "Run!" or "Don't go into the basement!" They are attempting to control the threat. If you are a horror movie fan, I'm sure you don't truly want to be chased by a masked man with a bloody butcher knife, but unconsciously you are energized by exposing yourself to threat knowing that you will prevail over the fear.

In Alfred Hitchcock's "The Birds," a small town is victim to aviary attack. The use of everyday people allows the viewer to relate to characters in the movie. Birds are typically non-threatening, innocuous creatures. They co-exist with the human species and, for most of us, birds do not rouse fear. Birds represent a control that exists between human beings and nature. The relationship between birds and humans in "The Birds" parallels the reality that tragedy can emerge from absolute calm.

Peter Benchley's "Jaws" provided a similar effect, though we innately fear sharks. Benchley's use of the ocean provided metaphor. At some level, we are aware there are things below the surface we opt to ignore, and the shark in "Jaws", like fear, crashed through when we were least expectant. Control was stolen, and we spent the rest of the movie vying to get control back. In the end, we walk out of the theater victorious over the fear into which we were submerged.

Biographies are about control, as well. True life stories don't follow the lives of individuals working for 40 years at Sears. Biographical movies are about survival or triumph over oppressive odds. The movie "Unbroken" reveals a man who survived overwhelming odds in World War II. The novel and film capture the spirit of our refusal to surrender to defeat. The movie is not about life or events but about deep fear, impending death and victory and control over death.

Smiles and laughter are contagious; both are basic forms of hypnotism. When your pet yawns when you are angry, he is unconsciously attempting to relax you. Yawning elicits physiological changes in others, and yawning is contagious. The next time you become angry with your pet, watch for the yawn unconsciously intended to relax you. Laughter is also contagious, and the physiological effect on others relaxes and deflects aggression.

Comedy and humor are deflections of fear. Our response to fear or bad news is sometimes "inappropriate" laughter. When I was 11, my friend was killed in a tragic accident. The situation was surreal, and when I first got the news I began to laugh. While I didn't understand at the time, the reaction was response to my fear and discomfort.

Several years later, as an adult, my sister broke into laughter at my aunt's funeral. She had just asked if the neck brace my cousin was wearing was due to a known attack on her by a boyfriend. When my aunt responded the neck brace had nothing to do with the attack but was secondary to a self-inflicted gunshot wound, my sister howled. The laughter was not about the injury but about my sister deflecting the pressured fear created by my cousin's difficulties and the underlying reality of sitting in a funeral home.

In the movie "Bridesmaids," Maya Rudolph plays Lillian, a socialite bride to be. While the movie is full of humor, the laughs are in response to fear of loss of control. When the future bride and bridesmaids go to a wedding dress store, after eating bad restaurant food, they begin to feel ill. Unable to locate a vacant restroom, Lillian runs across the street in hopes of finding another lavatory. She is unable to get to the other side of the street. She slowly squats in the middle of the congested avenue, the purely white dress she is wearing billowing around her, and defecates in front of the world.

The scene draws raucous laughter from the crowd. The reality of her situation, however, is horrifying. The character and, therefore, the audience experiences overwhelming humiliation and loss of control of bodily function. Thus, in this comedic situation, the protagonist is struck with a social tragedy, but the fear of loss of control is defended by humor.

While many speak of irony as the foundation of comedy, the true, underlying hinge is fear of loss of control – namely social control.

Several years ago, when I was driving my 12 year old daughter to school on a cold, wintery day, and she was staring blankly out the window in refusal to fully wake, she screamed in laughter. As we drove past the gas station, I saw the object of her glee. A man of about 30 was clinging to the side-step of his lifted pick-up truck, his boots working against the ice beneath him, he trying to regain his footing. "His feet went right out from under him," she laughed, now wide awake. "He shot underneath his truck."

All movies are sublimation of our fear and illusion of control. From horror to drama, the theme is controlling or confronting the fear of losing control. And the real fear is death. An effective movie leaves audiences changed for a period of time, either uplifted and feeling in control or down and sad when loss is the theme. Emotions stem from fear, the catalyst for attempting control.

Theme parks provide us opportunity to get even closer to fear, while maintaining control. It really doesn't make sense that many of us climb onto roller-coasters and allow ourselves to be jerked around in the air for several minutes – unless you consider the quandary we have with fear and control. Why would we allow ourselves to be strapped into a cart and taken to speeds exceeding 100 mph? Why would we endure one of our greatest and oldest fears, falling from the sky and then being ripped from gravitational pull and shot to heights of skyscrapers – unless we are attempting to face our fear while given the security of being safe? Of having control?

Haunted houses exact the same response. We walk through a darkened space, while creatures and faux mass murderers jump out at us, chain saws screaming in our direction and ghouls jumping from corners. We are paralleling the feeling of being faced with death and then walking away, in control.

Our fear of death invokes the drive to control. Because we deny our mortality, the reality of the threat of death, we are mostly unaware of our compensatory need to control, to mitigate our lack of control. However, as with all drives that are suppressed or otherwise defended, there is seepage of the unconscious into the conscious; so the information is mostly hidden and then sublimated.

NEW YORK

My mother grew up during the Great Depression. In the early 1940's, following the attack on Pearl Harbor, she watched her future husband, her brother and so many friends get sent overseas. The nation was impoverished and was now placing all meager resources into the war effort. Young men were fighting, women were taking over the factory jobs, and the disenfranchised were still digging through trash cans looking for a meal. But there was still hope.

After the War, when daylight began to emerge and warm our nation, national optimism swelled. My mom and her brother, just home from the Navy, drove, on the spur of the moment, to New York City and arrived in Times Square at midnight.

When she tells the story today, her blue eyes smile and sharpen. She takes a deep breath. She had lived and worked in Detroit, but New York was fantastic. Towering buildings, rising into the clouds. It was like nothing she'd seen, nothing she could have imagined. The architecture was foreboding, breathtaking, awe-inspiring. They were just buildings, but the memory they implanted years ago are still with her. They were powerful and fantastic; the City made her feel as though anything was possible.

CHAPTER EIGHT

ARCHITECTURE

Architects give us temples in which something marvelous is obviously going on. Actually, practically nothing is going on.

-Kurt Vonnegut

On September 11, 2001, terrorists hijacked planes and flew them into the World Trade Center in New York City. The reason the towers were the target is no mystery; the World Trade Center was a symbol of control. The towers were located in the financial district of New York City, the most fiscally powerful place on the planet. The Towers, when completed, were the tallest buildings in the world. The cost of the buildings (in 2015 American dollars) exceeded $2 billion. The City and the buildings were projections of strength and power. The terrorists, in an attempt to exert control, demolished the symbol. Additional targets were the Pentagon, housing the Department of Defense, and the Capitol Building. These buildings were the physical icons of American control, and Al-Qaeda undertook to destroy them.

The architecture of the world, the societies we build, is reflection of our collective foundation and conscience. Architecture projects our need to control, and the evidence is everywhere. While the world is more metaphysical than concrete, we lay down our sense of reality in physical terms. We build temples to represent spirituality and art to reflect our emotions.

Skyscrapers continue to get taller. As the East vies for more economic and political control, structures in that part of the world are stretching higher. Currently, the tallest building on record in the world is Burj Khalifa in Dubai, United Arab Emirates at 2,717 feet and 163 floors. The second tallest is the Shanghai Tower in Shanghai, China. It rises 2,073 feet with 121 floors. While it is deftly argued that skyscrapers are not all about ego and are more about wisely using land space, skyscrapers are clearly about assertion of control and strength. Were it only about prodigious use of space, spires and antennae to extend the height would not be so important, world record competition would not be engaged and nations vying for more control would not be contracting with companies to build the tallest, most ominous buildings on earth. There is nothing inherently wrong with expressing control through architecture, but it is important to recognize it for what it is.

Towering buildings are not the only indication our physical, social design is an expression of our drive to be in control. Expressions of architecture compete with controls in nature. As a species, we build enormous homes on beaches, at the edges of powerful oceans and on the sides of eroding cliffs. We build cities on brackish swamps, and we span bridges across bays and keys. The engineering feats are amazing, spectacular, but also indication of our need to manipulate the environment and to demonstrate our ability to control the forces of nature.

China is attempting to gain more control worldwide. The Chinese military is substantial, and its business and industry are evolving, exponentially. The Chinese expression of need to control is also evidenced in architecture. China has 5 of the 10 largest expansion bridges in the world, and China has plans to build Sky City, which when completed will be the tallest building in the world, at 2,749 feet.

Akashi-Kaikyo Bridge in Kobe, Japan, is currently the longest suspension bridge in the world, stretching 12,828 feet or nearly two and a half miles and equal to the length of about eight Sears Towers. The two towers on the bridge, at nearly 100 stories, make the bridge the tallest in the world. As such, it is the longest, tallest and most expensive suspension bridge in the world. The site is an area of the world with the most tumultuous, ravaging storms and seas. Tsunamis, hurricanes and driving winds make the waterway treacherous. Human psyche does not seek to figure a way around, but a way to control the fury of nature. William Starrett, a skyscraper builder, said, "Building skyscrapers is the nearest peace-time equivalent of war."

Architecture screams our earthly need to control. From the nearly 5,000 year old Khufuís Pyramid, which until the 20th Century, was the tallest building on Earth, to the skyscrapers of today, man has erected great monuments. Some of the greatest structures have been religious symbols, calling attention to centers of omnipotent control. St. Basil's Cathedral, built in the 14th Century in the Red Square in Moscow, was one of the most remarkable structures of its time. Ivan the Terrible ordered the construction and, when it was complete, legend holds Ivan ordered the architects eyes removed so that he could not replicate the architectural feat.

Architecture is an art, rising from our unconscious. The buildings of the past and of today reflect our deepest fears and aspirations for control. Architecture is the physical projection of our inner selves, and it demonstrates clearly our need to assert and proclaim control. As such, edification of control by some will lead to destruction by others. Destruction is the simplest form of control, and the most infantile. We have all seen a toddler in destructive mode. Terrorism is essentially an adult tantrum, overcompensation for fear of inability to provide constructive control. Ruination is the most immediate expression of power.

Everything we collectively build is a projection of our unconscious world. Just as art displays our inner feelings and thoughts, buildings and structure provide windows into our internal universe. Our need to control, to prove our ability and might, is reflected in the mansions sitting on hilltops and towers stretching into the stratosphere with the extended antennae and spires.

Medieval castles were built on high bluffs and cliffs to effect the greatest defensive strategy. The positioning of the kingdoms was an effort to literally control and fend-off death. The aerial view allowed better perspective and vigilance. Buildings today provide more symbolic control, the elevation representing the power. The result is the same, however; both provide dissipation of fear through assertion of control. There is irony in the building of homes on shores and at the edges of powerful rivers, or on the sides of mountains or in the lowest lying marshlands. Nearly everyone wants the view of the ocean, the river or majestic mountains. We feel most relaxed when taking in the awe of grand mountain ranges or the expanse of an ocean view; and that is because of the unconscious knowledge that nature is in control. We want to let go and be taken care of, but we are driven to try to control.

BUGS BUNNY

Yosemite Sam advances on Bugs Bunny in a desert setting. “Stop walking you doggone, long eared galoot.”

Bugs, paws on waist, “Just a minute, partner. You can’t talk to me like that. Them is fightin’ words.”

“Theeeeeeeem is fightin’ words,” Sam bellows.

“I dare you to step over that line.” Bugs Bunny drags a line in the sand with his foot.

Sam steps over the line. “Okay, I’m steppin’.”

Bugs makes another line. “I dare you to step over this one.”

Sam aggresses over the line.

“This one.” Bugs continues backing up, dragging lines in the sand.

“This one. This one. That one. This one.”

Sam proceeds stepping over the lines, and following the final line, Bugs steps out of the way. Sam walks over the edge of a cliff, falling about a hundred feet. Dust billows on impact.

Bugs Bunny and his crew of outrageous characters were foundational for many of us who grew up in the sixties and early seventies. The artwork was vivid, the characters deep and the plot clear: destroy one another.

PART THREE

DESTRUCTION

CHAPTER NINE

VIOLENCE

An eye for an eye will only make the whole world blind.

-Mahatma Gandhi

Not all people who lose control will resort to violence, but violence is always the result of attempting to gain control. Violence is assertion of control. When there is no known alternative to quell fear, violence becomes control. Homicide and suicide are always about control.

When individuals lose hope and believe there is no other opportunity to regain control, there is always great risk of violence. Erika Strom was a 28 year old woman who worked as a cashier at a grocery store. She graduated second of 245 students from her high school, where she was a cheerleader and queen of homecoming. After high school she attended community college but, at age 21, became pregnant with her boyfriend's baby. Don Franklin was a diesel mechanic. He played high school football and, following high school, attended a mechanic's certification course.

Erika's friends thought she would leave the area to realize her dreams, but most believed Don was destined to stay in the same town. Erika's best friend, Tonya said, "Erika was bright and alive and wanted to swallow the world up. He (Don) was simple. He wasn't bright like Erika, and he was constantly on her, because I think he was afraid of losing her."

Don began drinking more, putting down a 12 pack of beer after work, almost nightly. He became verbally aggressive with Erika, and there is suggestion he was physical with her. On the night of Erika's death, Don backhanded their child, David, then 7. Erika had threatened to leave before, but this time she was packing. And Don snapped. He later said he was only trying to scare Erika when he pointed the gun at her.

Relationships that end in homicide end because the perpetrator fears losing everything and takes everything. Individuals who lose partial control may yell and some become violent. But when all hope is lost, when there appears to be imminent emotional death for the perpetrator, homicide is the extreme reaction that momentarily restores control.

Homicide-suicide, while it may appear contrary, is another extreme and desperate grasp for control. Taking life demonstrates omnipotence.

In 2008, in Michigan's sparsely populated upper peninsula, Scott Johnson fatally shot three teens at a pond where the teens were swimming. He had never met them. Johnson, in his mid-thirties, was long unemployed and living with his mother. He was being pursued by police following an alleged sexual assault. Johnson went into the woods to an area he called his safe place; "It was the only place that let me feel like I was in control." He donned camouflage clothing, armed himself with a .308 semi-automatic rifle and began shooting the first people he saw. Johnson's fear was fueled by an impending arrest and a life of having little control; now he had lost all control and attempted to take it back through random, extreme violence.

Individuals with perfectionist personalities suggest higher levels of fear and greater need to control. Tyler was a high school senior is his final semester, attending a prestigious private high school. He was captain of the football team, ran track and received only A's on report cards since beginning the school at the start of 9th grade. In March he had already been accepted to the University of Michigan on a full academic scholarship. His girlfriend of a year and a half had been accepted to another university, and following a disagreement between the two, she broke off their relationship. He went home after school, unlocked his father's gun cabinet and lethally shot himself with a 9mm pistol.

Tyler was higher risk than normal for teen suicide, though few were aware. A student who does not feel compulsion to be completely in control all the time is healthier and less at risk. Individuals who strive for perfection become so terrified with not controlling they believe they have failed. Some assert control at an ultimate level and take life.

In the slew of school shootings that have stained our world, the perpetrators who have killed have taken extreme control. Most perpetrators believe others have bullied them or that they have been denied social status. While many students feel bullied and ostracized, the vast majority do not kill. Individuals who see hope of controlling their lives through other means, who do not feel entirely dejected, rejected and without control don't commit homicide. When hope is drained, when deep depression sets in and there is no belief control can be attained, individuals are at far greater risk of violence, either to themselves, others or both.

Recently, in a suburb of Detroit, Brian White, an enraged 19 year old white male, went to the house of his ex-girlfriend, who had just broken off their relationship. The couple had dated through high school, and when the relationship ended, White made many attempts at reversing the break-up. He called his ex-girlfriend incessantly, but she thwarted his attempts at reconciliation. His world was ending. His life wouldn't be the same without the girlfriend with whom he had spent the past several years. The rage was based in fear, as rage always is; White was petrified at the thought of losing his girlfriend. His inability to look past the situation and into the future, his lack of creative problem solving, left him with a view that his world was done. White saw the ending as literal; and he asserted the maximum level of control. He first cut out (with the sharp blade of an axe) the individuals he judged were facilitating his demise, namely his girlfriend's mother and the new boyfriend. He tied his ex-girlfriend up and tortured her, as he believed she had been psychologically torturing him. In the end, she lived; her mother and new boyfriend were dead. And while White did end his world that day, he momentarily was in control; through an immature and destructive method, he took charge.

Violence is control expressed at its most desperate level. In movies, violence and destruction are trite ways of tapping viewers' emotions for control. But in reality, acts of destruction and violence are indicative of an individual's losing the battle for control. Destruction of property is an immediate (and primitive) way of controlling. Destruction is based in anger, and anger is always based in fear…fear of losing something or someone…and ultimately of death. Anger both masks fear and provides fuel for control.

When an individual is in relative control, he tends to be calm. Yelling and throwing things are associated with someone out of control. When a man strikes out, he is not in control. So, a person labeled controlling is, in fact, out of control and attempting to re-gain control.

Panic, of course, is evidence of lack of control. A sound plan will take panic out of a situation, because a plan is a road map, a guide to dealing with a situation. When a plan is being followed, the frontal lobe is engaged; in panic the frontal lobe is essentially disengaged and the limbic system is in full gear – we are back to the animal level of operation. If you've ever heard recordings of an airline pilot in an emergency situation, you have a sense of how a sound plan precludes panic. In recent years, Captain Chesley Sullenberger III of US Airways landed a passenger airliner on the Hudson River in New York City. Captain Sullenberger had a sound plan, founded on years of emergency preparation. He did not simply make a decision at the time he was putting the plane on the river; he had 29 years of flight experience with the airlines and was an Air Force fighter pilot before. He had practiced emergency situations, he was adept at flying, and he had faith, a foundational belief, in a plan. He didn't panic. He spoke calmly with the tower and deftly put the plane down, wheels up, in the Hudson River.

A plan constitutes faith. You have a map, and you have confidence in the map. Faith can be secular, spiritual or religious. True faith mitigates need to control, because control is being managed through a higher level or in deference to a greater plan.

John Peoples was a fire fighter in a large university town in the mid-west. He had 23 years with the department. He was respected in his community by friends, acquaintances and family. His identity, the foundation from which he lived and the life-faith to which he was connected, was his position as a lieutenant and supervisor for the department. While he may not have consciously thought about respect and position as means of control, it was his base. Few knew, however, that John Peoples had a growing problem with binge drinking. As the Michigan economy grew worse and the tax base narrowed, municipalities laid off firefighters and police. Fear of loss ate at John. On a night in December 2011, John got into an argument with his wife about money. And he struck her. In his blind rage he hit her, and the trauma she incurred resulted in her hospitalization. He drove his vehicle onto a highway, pulled to the side of the road, left a letter on the passenger seat then stepped in front of a semi-truck, taking his life. As a compensation for his dramatic loss of control, he took ultimate control.

Gangs, like terrorist groups, are complicated systems, yet fairly primitive. If you don't belong you are an enemy. And enemies are kept out of the circle. In Detroit, there is a one square mile area between 7 and 8 Mile Roads in which men in their late teens and early twenties were more likely to die of a gunshot wound than if they had served in Afghanistan at the height of the war. The men defend their territory and kill others who cross the road dividing the drawn lines. It's all about fear – fear of not being in control, terror of losing control. The more the threat of death approaches, the more volatile and violent man becomes. Control is everything. And any measure will be taken to maintain control.

Fast cars exude power, and driving lifts primitive control closer to the surface. If you're in the enveloping leather seat of an Aston Martin, power is transferred to your toes, and it feels invincible. But when we are driving, and someone cuts us off, threatens us, the animal inside may emerge. Fear gives quickly to aggression. The primitive, control- drive shuts down logic and reasoning. An estimated 1,500 drivers are seriously injured or killed each year due to "road-rage." The unconscious need to control, if not consciously checked, can have devastating results.

While history of aggression and violence is the best predictor of a person being violent in the future, the newspapers are full of perpetrators who murder and have no history of such behavior. If there is hopelessness the threat of violence always rises. If there is a childhood history of loss or abandonment, the threat level rises higher still. Children who experienced abandonment are more likely to have an immature emotional reaction to loss, and the loss is more likely to trigger a more powerful fear of loss of complete control. Fear and control are the yin and yang; the greater the perceived loss the greater the need to take control.

SCHOOL MASSACRE

The most devastating school massacre in United States history did not occur at Columbine, Paducah or Sandy Hook. It happened in the small town of Bath, Michigan in 1927.

Andrew Kehoe was treasurer of the school board, a county clerk and farmed an 80 acre spread just outside the town of about 300. But Kehoe was not a man in control, and despite his efforts to hold it all together, it was beginning to come apart. Known for his thrift and controlling ways, his world tilted when his house fell into foreclosure, his wife grew increasingly ill, he lost his seat as county clerk and lost the battle to stop a school building tax increase.

Andrew Kehoe was born in a farming community in southern Michigan. He had twelve siblings, and when his mother died during his early childhood his father remarried a woman with whom Kehoe did not get along. They argued often. When the oil stove blew up in the kitchen and engulfed his stepmother in flames, 14 year old Kehoe looked on for a few minutes before dousing her with water. She died of her injuries, and while there was inquiry, Kehoe was never charged.

On May 18, 1927 Kehoe murdered his wife. At about 8:45 a.m. he blew up his house and several outbuildings, which he had packed with explosives. Almost simultaneously, he detonated dynamite and pyrotol he had hidden in the school he was supposed to be serving, killing 36 children and two adults. As rescuers rushed to the scene, Kehoe used a rifle to set off more explosives, killing the superintendent, the post master, his father-in-law and himself. All told, the casualties included 45 dead, 38 of whom were elementary children, and 58 injured. Kehoe had taken control.

CHAPTER TEN

TERRORISM

We are effectively destroying ourselves by violence masquerading as love.

-R. D. Laing

Terrorism is the act or threat of violence. It is coercive, a threat or action used to control the behavior of others. Terrorists, and terrorist groups, believe they have virtually no control, unless through coercive, violent means. Anger and resentment at not having control is at the heart of terrorists' needs to manipulate by making others feel that same sense of terror at feeling powerless.

Psychologically, this is a defensive mechanism, a reaction formation. There is despair and rage about not enjoying the prosperity others are perceived to have so, according to Laurence Miller, terrorists label such lifestyles "evil, unholy excrescences of Western decadence, to be expunged and destroyed."

Terrorism exists where individuals feel they have no hope of control through other means. Violence is always about control, and terrorism is an overt response to the fear of not being able to control. Absent military power, terrorists instill terror in the masses by exercising fear through limited strikes.

Terrorism is fundamentally a bullying tactic, a means of controlling through intimidation and threat. Bullying occurs in schools, the workplace and in homes. Regardless the environment, bullies use intimidation to control others' behaviors to mitigate fear of not having control. The bully in a school is more likely to possess inferior language skills, and so he uses the less sophisticated manipulation of threat. Terrorists, likewise, belong to groups with no political voice.

Children with autism, by diagnosis, exhibit speech and language deficits and deficits in decoding others' body language and facial expressions. Consequently, children with autism have a higher than average aggressive response. They are less able to modulate control through language and expression, so the child strikes out with developmentally regressive behaviors like biting and clawing.

Mr. Bower was an administrator in a district with a program for students with autism. He had been through the school on a number of occasions, but Bower was not regularly on site. Wearing a suit and a colorful tie, he walked down the hallway toward the principal's office. He gave little thought to the 16 year old student who stood up from the drinking fountain and regarded him. Bower was stunned then staggered when the student charged him and punched him in the jaw. The 16 year old, Jack, was non-verbal. Ties were provocative to Jack. He couldn't talk about it, though it is fair to assume ties symbolized threat. All the employees in the building knew about Jack's rage response to ties – so ties were not allowed in the building. Unfortunately, nobody had informed Mr. Bower.

Understanding issues of control with terrorists and bullies is important in attempting to strategize methods of mitigating violent behavior. Those without a voice, who feel no control, will react with a fear response - avoiding or aggressing.

It is difficult to be objective about the September 11, 2001 attack on the twin towers in New York City. Acts of terrorism are so emotionally charged. For many, the violence on that day was personal. But even for those not directly involved, the action on America was a direct hit. It rocked each and every one of us.

Every day, some act of violence occurs somewhere in America and certainly in the world. Some stories tug at our emotions more than others. As human beings, most of us empathize with others when they are in pain. But the closer the story is to us, the greater the effect. A mother who hears about a family burned in a home will likely carry the images in her heart and mind longer than will someone who has no children. A story about an airliner going down evokes emotion in nearly all of us, because nearly all of us fly. The closer you are to actually having flown or being about to fly, the greater the reaction.

The 911 attack on New York hit everyone directly, because it threatened each person in the nation. We view New York (whether you love or hate the City) as a cornerstone of America. It is the seat of our cosmopolitan personality, the gateway through which many of our ancestors passed, and New York represents a segment of the control that we, as a nation, enjoy. New York is the Big Apple, the town of opportunity, the location where bigger than life things happen and bigger than life people reside. It is the city of stars and finance and law and creativity. It is a city of control. The act of terrorism delivered a blow to the City and our nation that took us, momentarily, to our knees.

Over 3,000 people died that day, yet everyday 3,000 people die in this nation. Of course, it's different. These people weren't supposed to die. These people were everyday citizens, in control of their lives, and without warning, with no real predictability, they perished.

One of the most disturbing aspects of terrorism is that it is not expected. It can happen anywhere, anytime to anyone. The power the terrorist has on society is that it cannot be predicted. The more predictable an action, the more control we have. That is why death is so frightening – its timing cannot be predicted. Remember the pilot putting down the plane? He could not change the fact calamity was imminent, but he had a plan and knew he was doing all he could. He was in control to the extent he could be. And that is powerful.

As a counter measure to the 911 attacks, the United States and other nations spend billions of dollars every year. We lost 3,000 lives on September 11, 2001, but the monetary response relative to the action has been financially overwhelming. We developed the Department of Homeland Security. We imposed controls on airlines, establishing check-points, created the TSA and launched counter-terrorism task forces in the FBI, CIA, branches of the military and in police departments across the country. We entered into a decade long war, on two fronts, wherein we lost 4,000 military personnel, sustained injury to tens of thousands of soldiers and expended nearly a billion dollars a month. Our nation, in part due to our position of needing to remain in control, nearly fell into financial ruin.

George Tenet, the CIA Director at the start of the 911 attacks, reduced the basis for the attacks to something less than violence. Tenet said that terrorism is propagated by conditions in which young males with little education, virtually no job prospects and minimal opportunity attempt to find a way to survive, to be (and to control). Those vulnerable to the call of terrorism are looking for a cause and sense of belonging. These are young men who have essentially no control or direction over their destinies. Their sense of futility is deep; and the attempt to control will match the intensity of their despair. At a compensatory level, fledgling terrorists are attempting to get control equal to or greater than their sense of lack of control. The result is significant. Damaging. Lack of opportunity and control in distant corners of the globe is an issue for all of us.

International terrorism is wildly complicated. Culture, religion, generational family dynamics, economic issues and prejudices are all ingredients. But the need to control in order to reduce fear and rage is always at play, and understanding that concept may help, at some level, to mitigate the atrocities caused by terrorism. Terrorism is borne of fear, and control is the compensatory behavior. Better understanding of control is a step in the direction of understanding terrorism, its causes and better ways of dealing with its tragic results.

BONNIE AND CLYDE

New York Daily News (*Excerpt*)

April 22, 1934 – BY VIRGIL S. BECK

Dallas, Tex., April 21

Officers call Barrow and his gun moll "a pair of human rats" who dash about the country like mad dogs, jeering, cursing and laughing diabolically at their dying victims. These same officers admit the bandits are experts with firearms and absolutely fearless, and doubt that they ever will be captured alive. They seem to know every highway and side road in the Middle West. They strike suddenly and ruthlessly, and when officers think they have the pair cornered they suddenly appear in another State. …

"Did you know who I was?"

When the officer admitted he did not, Barrow replied:

"It's a good thing. Seven like you did, and they're pushing up daisies now." …

Meanwhile, Barrow, with the blood of at least nine men on his hands; his gun moll, Bonnie Parker, drinker of strong corn whisky and smoker of strong cigar, and Raymond Hamilton, fugitive from a 263-year prison sentence, dash over the highways from the Canadian border to the Gulf, robbing, looting, and ready to kill at the least provocation.

CHAPTER ELEVEN

MURDER VIOLENCE RETROSPECT

We rob banks!

-Bonnie Parker

Murder occurs when other avenues of control are unavailable. Homicide is desperate fear, at base level. It also is as old as humankind.

The Great Depression was the worst economic time in the history of the nation. It is argued that crime rises during difficult economic times because there is little employment. But, not everybody breaks the law when the economy tanks. The reason crime increases is because people are attempting to regain control. Those more anxious and having less faith (in government, God or any other entity) are more likely to break the law.

If the hypothesis that control is a reaction to fear of death is correct, and if control is a drive countering fear, society should see significant increases in desperate attempts to over-control when economics turn down. During the 1930's, one of the most financially oppressive times in modern history, crime skyrocketed. Prohibition, a social measure attempting to control human behavior, met pushback from bootleggers and backwoods still operators who ran illegal liquor trades. Money was scarce, so a plethora of bank robbers emerged. During the 1930's, the list of bank robbers, thieves and gang members wanted by the FBI included Ma Barker; the Barker gang; Bonnie and Clyde; George "Machine Gun" Kelly; Pretty Boy Floyd; "Killer" Burke of the Valentine's Day Massacre; John Dillinger; Francis "2 Gun" Kelly who was in a two hour shootout with police, in front of 15,000 bystanders, before his arrest; and George "Baby Face" Nelson. These characters lived nearly 100 years ago, but they are still recognizable to most of us today.

If murder is the result of fear occurring when control is lost, it would reason homicides should increase when other aspects of perceived control decrease. In studies of economic change, murder does increase when the economy sours. When there is less wage equity across society, homicide rates and violence go up.

Because economic shifts are relatively common over time, there is some expectation the markets, both financial and job based, will climb and fall. There is predictability, and predictability is key to feeling in control. So, some ebb and flow of the economy is expected, and therefore people are moderately patient with an up and down economy for awhile.

The social effect, then, is that you don't see immediate negative reaction at a societal level when the market shows blips. The job market was tough back in the 1980's, and we came out just fine. In fact, the 90's brought an economic boon. That is the mindset. However, when the economy continues to decline, when job loss soars unabated, when housing foreclosures hit levels only reached during the Great Depression and the GNP shows decline quarter after quarter, the collective sense is this is not predictable. We don't know where this is going. If it isn't predictable, we are not in control.

The volatility of the 2016 presidential race is not surprising if you consider the fear rising in the masses, due to the prolonged economic stall. We seek vicarious control through leaders, and some are adept at exploiting fears and promising control through absurd bravado. In economic crises, we see signs of over-control or of compensatory control. Crime increases, because those who are most vulnerable to slight economic downturns begin to take what they want by force or try to control their intimate worlds more aggressively. Domestic violence increases, theft rises and home invasions peak.

Bonnie Parker and Clyde Barrow were labeled by federal law authorities cold-blooded, murderous bank robbers. They ran a spree of crime across the mid-west, killing police officers and anyone else who got in their way. Bonnie, Clyde and the Barrow gang are credited with murdering at least 13, and yet the public perception of the couple was mostly positive.

While not all citizens reacted with criminality during the Great Depression, a large number cheered criminals on. They lived vicariously through the bank robbers and bootleggers. At some level, they agreed with, and were excited by, the actions of people who refused to relinquish control. The criminals became celebrities. That may explain why twenty-thousand people attended Bonnie Parker's funeral. She was a folk hero, because she refused to acquiesce to the oppressive machinations of the government. She asserted herself, attempting to control outcomes.

In a study of men who murder wives, all convicted killers revealed they were trying to maintain control and feared loss of control. Researchers concluded, "The participants gave the murder various meanings; however, the common one was the idea that through eliminating the woman they would be able to overcome their sense of helplessness and regain control of their lives." While the researchers cite many other studies and conclusions in studies, issues of control were always present, without regard to educational achievement, income, psychiatric label or history of violence.

One of the convicted murderers in the Aldarondo study reflected, "She had a lot of power over me. She knew how to manipulate me like a puppet on strings. She got what she wanted. I was like a puppet in her hands." The man clearly believed he had no control, and he attributed his wife with usurping his control. His fear was so great he eliminated her. Another convict noted, prior to killing his wife, "I realized that suddenly all the plans I had collapsed one after another." If nothing ever works out as planned, there is no control. If you cannot predict there is no sense of stability.

Loss of love is always connected to loss of control. Fear is the base emotion, and love is relative absence of fear. Love is feeling safe and protected. Love is antithetical to fear.

Men who kill their spouses have a poorer foundational sense of control. As children, they likely had little to no safety net, nobody to protect them from fears. Neglected children over-control by hoarding food, clinging to others in adult relationships and sometimes engaging in other compulsive behaviors like drug and alcohol addictions. Neglected children appear controlling because they fear they have no foundational control. Men who killed their spouses revealed early childhood experiences included abandonment, neglect, or physical abuse along with parental rejection, hostility, lack of supervision, and lack of boundaries.

Researcher Malach-Pines noted, "When a mother is consistent, stable, trustworthy and sensitive to the needs of an infant, the child will develop a sense of confidence and develop healthy intimate relationships. However, when a mother abandons or rejects a baby, the individual is bound to develop, as an adult, anxiety and/or ambivalence with regard to love. He might choose to avoid the risks involved with intimate relationships, altogether."

Taking a life, through homicide or suicide, is the ultimate control. Omnipotent control. If our unconscious level of control is at a negative 1, we assert compensatory control at a positive one. If our loss is at negative 100, we lunge forward, desperately grasping for control. Murder is the result of that sometimes desperate grasp.

THE RIPPER

Dear Boss,

I keep on hearing the police have caught me but they wont fix me just yet. I have laughed when they look so clever and talk about being on the right track. That joke about Leather Apron gave me real fits. I am down on whores and I shant quit ripping them till I do get buckled. Grand work the last job was. I gave the lady no time to squeal. How can they catch me now. I love my work and want to start again. You will soon hear of me with my funny little games. I saved some of the proper red stuff in a ginger beer bottle over the last job to write with but it went thick like glue and I cant use it. Red ink is fit enough I hope ha. ha. The next job I do I shall clip the ladys ears off and send to the police officers just for jolly wouldn't you. Keep this letter back till I do a bit more work, then give it out straight. My knife's so nice and sharp I want to get to work right away if I get a chance. Good Luck.

Yours truly

Jack the Ripper

Dont mind me giving the trade name

CHAPTER TWELVE

SEXUAL MURDER

You feel the last bit of breath leaving their body. You're looking into their eyes. A person in that situation is God!

-Theodore Bundy

Sexual assault is raw control, and it underscores the propensity for violence in human beings. When fear of loss of control turns outward into rage, human beings can exact horrible destruction upon one another. Rape is about sex, but moreover, rape is about control. There are components of control in all aspects of sex, but rape is a violent force. The rapist controls the victim, literally subduing and implanting himself. Sometimes he hurts the victim, not necessarily because it is critical to completion of the act of rape, but because he wants to control the victim's emotions and physical response. Rapists sometimes murder, the ultimate act of control, a god-like imposition on another.

Theodore Bundy raped and murdered at least 35 women across several states during the 1970's. Some estimate he killed more than 100. Outwardly, Bundy presented as a controlled and relatively quiet individual. In fact, his demeanor of control and his projected confidence lured women into his web. He was anything but controlled, however.

Bundy was purported to be an only child. His mother, Eleanor Cowell, was 15 when Bundy was born, and there is no definitive record of who his father was. There has been speculation his father was also his maternal grandfather. Ted and his mother lived with his maternal grandparents for his first three years. Bundy was led to believe his grandparents were his parents, and he was told his mother was his older sister. He and his mother moved when he was 3, and she later married. The Bundy's had 4 children together, and his stepfather adopted Ted.

While Bundy's murderous and sexual rage was grounded largely in his sociopathic personality, the feral need to over-control was due to his inability to trust and develop empathetic relationships, which is the deepest root of sociopathy. An attachment to another human being, typically a mother, builds trust and establishes a sense he will be taken care of by an adult.

In 1967, Ted Bundy began dating Stephanie Brooks, a co-ed at the University of Washington. Brooks was described as an attractive, white female with long, brown hair parted down the middle. A year later, when Bundy dropped out of college, Brooks broke up with him, calling him immature and without drive. She implied he was not a mature adult in control of his life and future. Bundy was devastated. Shortly after, disillusioned, he made his way back to his hometown in Pennsylvania. While there, he searched through details and public records of his family; it was then he learned, consciously anyway, his sister was really his mother.

Brook's break-up with Bundy, coupled with the underlying information about his family, rocked him. There was no safety net, nothing bonding him or supporting him. He was completely without foundation.

Bundy attempted to take control of his life. He re-enrolled in Washington University, where he performed exceptionally, earning a bachelor's degree in 1972. He was accepted to law school in 1973. Shortly thereafter, he sought out Stephanie Brooks, the girlfriend who had dumped him.

She was taken by his turn-around and impressed with his drive and direction. They dated and discussed marriage.

In January 1974, Bundy broke all contact with Brooks. When she finally reached him a month later and asked for an explanation, he said he had no idea what she was talking about. She had pulled the rug from beneath him, destroying his world, a couple years before. Now, he was destroying hers. And he would continue to destroy the lives of others for the remainder of his life outside prison walls. Bundy was no longer the victim; he was in control of victimizing others.

Bundy's first confirmed attack occurred about one month after the break-up with Brooks, when he broke into the basement apartment of Karen Shapiro, bludgeoning her unconscious and raping and sodomizing her with a speculum. She survived the attack but lived with lasting injuries. From that point forward, until his arrest, Bundy engaged in a spree of rapes, murders, mutilations, necrophilia and cannibalism on an approximate monthly interval. Shapiro, like nearly all Bundy's victims, resembled his girlfriend Stephanie Brooks. In terrified, determined rage, Bundy played God and snuffed out others' lives. Even when his victims were dead, Bundy came back to crime scenes, continuing to control and sexually manipulate and sometimes devour the cadavers.

It is not uncommon for serial killers to be raised by adoptive parents. (It is, however, rare for children raised by adoptive parents to become serial killers.) All things conscious are reflections of the unconscious. Adults who were not terrified about being abandoned and neglected feel there is foundational control. Neglected, abandoned and distrustful children must always be in control.

Anti-social Personality Disorder makes the control drive more dangerous, but it also provides insight into how the drive manifests. One of the hallmark aspects of a sociopath is the relative absence of a conscience, that moral compass that exists in the majority of human beings. In decision making, in most human beings, judgments are filtered through the conscience. We make decisions, taking into account our moral code and our sense of what is right and wrong. When we are enraged, however, that part of the brain may be circumvented. Crimes of passion, or temporary insanity, are legal explanations for this psychological/neurological function. The premise is that in some circumstances, typically surrounding a jilted lover, a partner may become enraged and commit a crime that would be outside the realm of his normal behavior. The courts typically look at rage, but rarely is the subject of intense fear considered, which is always at the foundation of rage. An insanity plea recognizes that sometimes the reasoning center of the brain short-circuits, and rage, or the need to control, is overwhelming. In the Anti-social Personality, however, conscience is essentially missing, so the control drive is much less mitigated.

There is always a component of anti-social personality that accompanies rape. Rapists are asserting control to compensate for terror of abandonment, of relational loss. They overcompensate by asserting complete control. All individuals who have substantial fear of abandonment don't rape, but all rapists are masking terror of abandonment through rage and control, in an unconscious compensatory strategy.

While it is easier for us, as a society, to label Bundy evil, that identification is dangerous, because it lets us off the hook. If he is evil, he is beyond our understanding, and we have no responsibility. The truth is Bundy is a product of us, of our society. He is what occurs when safety nets are gone, when foundations of trust are not established. Monsters are not conceived in a vacuum. We create the monsters. When we do not establish a foundation, a level of trust and concern, fear will create need for omnipotent control.

The need to better understand how fear and control propagates violence is a social concern. When we understand an issue, we can begin to treat the issue. As long as the dynamics of violence, due to fear and attempts to control, are not considered, understanding of how to deal with such violence is unlikely.

CHAPTER THIRTEEN

SUICIDE

Suicide is a form of murder – premeditated murder.

-Susann Kaysen

Suicide is devastating and seemingly senseless for those left behind. The act of suicide is violent, but it is an act of desperation resulting from a sense of complete loss of control, culminating with an individual taking all control.

People who end their lives by suicide are typically depressed, and the depression is most often biochemical; there is a genetic and biological component, often with a family history of depression or bipolar disorder. Sometimes the depression is situational – a series of devastating events lead to hopelessness, though there is often still a predisposition to the depressive hopelessness.

Often, thoughts of suicide are about removing oneself from a very bad situation. There is the idea or fantasy of peace and avoidance of the conflict or crisis at hand, and suicide provides option for the out. Talk of suicide should always be taken as a critical call out that could, through purposeful attempt or accident, result in death. The underlying issue, however, is control – or sense of having no control.

Williams and Pollack compared depressed, suicidal people with a group of depressed people who were not suicidal. Distinct factors separated the groups. The research found that individuals with clinical depression who are at significantly higher risk of attempting suicide have three cognitive characteristics in common:

1. Signals of Defeat – Individuals possess a hypersensitivity to issues of defeat, and the perception of their 'loser' status jumps out in front of all other information.

2. Being Trapped – Patients cannot get beyond the sense there is no way out, therefore, they do not look for solutions, because they feel there are none.

3. Absence of Rescue Factors – Individuals who attempt suicide do not believe there is any help coming. They are alone in the problem, which they see no way around.

Through brain imaging Van Heeringen found that suicidal patients exhibit problems with neurological receptors responsible for hopelessness and behavioral inhibition. In a separate study, Meyer found that certain dysfunctional attitudes, such as negative views of oneself, the world and the future are associated with these same receptors.

While these characteristics for suicidal ideation may not be surprising, it is noteworthy that in a group of people with clinical depression, the three collective suicide markers are found only in those who attempt suicide. And all the characteristics underscore fears of loss of control. Defeat is not about being challenged, it is about the obliteration of opportunity for success. Being trapped epitomizes loss of control. The belief there is no likelihood of rescue indicates the individual has no faith beyond himself; there is no net of control. Suicide is a last ditch attempt to end the agony by taking control back.

On October 1, 2014, a day after her newlywed husband's birthday, Brittany Maynard took an overdose of the sedative Secobarbital, in order to end her life. She was a pretty, twenty-nine year old, an only child and a recently married woman with dreams of travel and raising a family. Shortly after her wedding, she was diagnosed with a brain tumor and given 10 years to live. Upon learning this, Maynard said, "When you're 29 years old, being told you have that kind of timeline still feels like being told you're going to die tomorrow."

Her statement, while understandable, underscores our denial regarding mortality. To a person in their 20's, 10 years seems an eternity. A 30 year old never sees herself as the 40 year old. Her defenses were cracked, and Brittany became aware of her mortality. After additional medical tests were run and doctors found more disease, her prognosis was reduced to a life expectancy of 6 months.

"I don't want to die, but I am dying," Brittany said in a People Magazine interview. "My [cancer] is going to kill me, and it's a terrible, terrible way to die. So to be able to die with my family with me, to have control over my own mind, which I would stand to lose."

Brittany moved with her family to Oregon, where legislation allows "Death with Dignity," a medically assisted suicide option. "There is not a cell in my body that is suicidal or that wants to die," she said. "I want to live. I wish there was a cure for my disease but there's not. … Being able to choose to go with dignity is less terrifying."

Brittany looked death in the face; she was unwilling to relinquish control. She began doing the things she wanted to do in her life. She learned all she could about the potential progression of the tumor then planned her course, based on doctors' predictions. She sought and succeeded in controlling what she could of her life, and she took control of the way she died.

Medical diagnoses take away control, and individuals want control back. Suicide rates double for individuals with diabetes and cancer. Suicide runs 5 times the rate of non-affected individuals where neurological disorders, like multiple sclerosis and spinal cord injuries, are present. People with uncontrolled seizures commit suicide at 25 times the average rate of non-seizure individuals. Not coincidentally, the diseases which rob people of the most control are those which drive people to take their own lives.

Suicide, like homicide, is the most aggressive measure of taking control. This appears to be a dichotomy, but it is not. Control is different from fear. Control mitigates fear. We use control as a means of denying death, because we are programmed to control to avoid death. If we are in control we cannot die. We become immortal in our defended, conscious brains. We are wired to control, and sometimes individuals take control by ending their lives. We do not look at a 10 year span of time and believe we are going to die; we look at 10 years as an eternity. Unless the defenses are torn away. Unless your doctor tells you your time on earth is finite and limited. Then ten years means you are mortal. When we believe we have no control, we dig in and try to regain control. When we believe we are controlling, we are dissipating fear. Suicide is sometimes that end.

PUPPETEERS

"The conscious and intelligent manipulation of the organized habits and opinions of the masses is an important element in democratic society. Those who manipulate this unseen mechanism of society constitute an invisible government which is the true ruling power of our country. ...We are governed, our minds are molded, our tastes formed, our ideas suggested, largely by men we have never heard of. This is a logical result of the way in which our democratic society is organized. Vast numbers of human beings must cooperate in this manner if they are to live together as a smoothly functioning society. ...In almost every act of our daily lives, whether in the sphere of politics or business, in our social conduct or our ethical thinking, we are dominated by the relatively small number of persons...who understand the mental processes and social patterns of the masses. It is they who pull the wires which control the public mind."

Edward L. Bernays, Propaganda

CHAPTER FOURTEEN

MANIPULATION

Almost all people are hypnotics.

-Charles Fort

Manipulation happens several times a day, in every area of life. People manipulate to get what they need. Manipulation is about controlling situations. Everyone manipulates; and manipulation is not necessarily a bad thing.

In an office setting, the most overt level of manipulation is threat. A supervisor might state or infer termination. That is a bald move towards manipulating another; but there are more effective and subtle ways.

A coy supervisor may build ego. "John, I know you're a great worker. Three years in a row you were top in sales in this office. There have been some issues that were hard to negotiate, but I have faith. I really need you to step up for the team this month. We need you, John. Badly."

A co-worker may smile, her eyes flirtatious. "Joe, can you get me into a meeting with Spencer." She lifts her face, slightly. Her lips purse almost imperceptibly. "Please."

Some manipulation is more insidious. A co-worker may ask you cover for him, because he hasn't been performing. An employee may attack management, because she wants the onus of blame to lie with managers, rather than the work force. Males and females may use sexuality to soften or re-direct the attention on an issue or a request. An employee may speak with great authority on a subject, in an effort to push through an agenda, based on her assertions.

I was recently contacted by an employee trying to control a situation through me. Larry called me, presenting a red herring issue, before touching on the real subject matter. He had learned there was a plan to move one of the newer managers into a higher level position. He was opposed, but that wasn't how the conversation started. He simply said, "What do you think about Ray's decision making lately?" Ray was my boss. "I know he thinks he's doing what's right, but has he even spoken with you about the decision?" Larry's angle here, his manipulation, was to bring me into his fold by asserting my boss hadn't conferred with me on the plan. The hook was set. When I indicated he had not spoken with me about the decision, Larry stated, "Why would he not? You're HR. You're the person with the overarching perspective on this? What is Ray thinking?" The manipulation potentially takes me out of Ray's camp and places me alongside Larry. He now believes he can work with me as an ally, against Ray.

On the continuum of manipulations, those induced by individuals with significant psychological damage are potentially most dangerous. The sociopath can get a young woman into his car or get the elderly person to part with life savings. The histrionic can suck all attention toward herself and deflect focus. But day to day, people manipulate to get the small things they need.

A friend recently told the story of riding in the passenger seat of his sister's car, when they were pulled over by a police officer. The officer asked the driver if she knew why she was being pulled over. The driver, to her brother's dismay, loudly moaned. When the alarmed officer asked if he should call an ambulance she said, no, she just needed to get home to her prescription medication. The officer suggested the passenger drive her home, and as her brother pulled away from the police car and back onto the road she said, "And that, Brother, is how it's done."

Manipulation goes back to the beginning of time. It is revealed in the Bible, in the Koran and it runs throughout our history books. It starts at a very young age and is part of our development. Manipulation is necessary to build the bond between child and adult. When a child cries, because he doesn't want to sleep or because he is hungry, he is manipulating the environment. When things go well, the mother comes to the child and reassures him. She feeds him. He learns he can control his environment, that he can manipulate outcomes. The child who is not answered, who is unsuccessful in manipulating the environment at this age, will perceive he has no control, and he will try to overcompensate.

There is not much research, surprisingly, on manipulation. Harvey Clare, a psychiatrist, wrote, "Everyone seems to know what is meant by manipulation, yet the term is omitted in the psychiatric dictionary." Clare suggests manipulation is an aggression using cleverness and deception to influence others into gratifying the aggressor. Clare believed manipulation was generally conscious, but not always.

Deception is not always necessary. When your teenaged child asks for money, for instance, you might ask about the request. Your question, of course, is really a statement suggesting you are in control. That is, I can choose to provide you money or I may choose not to, depending on the purpose of the loan – or provision. When your child indicates the money is for beer, you say, um, no. She says, "I'm kidding, Daddy. I need gas money."

"I gave you money for gas a couple days ago. Does your boyfriend Ben ever help out with the gas?"

"Ben helped me pay for books this semester, so I don't want to be asking him for money all the time. And I ran your other daughter, Jessica, to Pom practice three times this week. That's why I don't have gas. I just need enough to get to school the next couple days."

"Here's forty," he says, emptying his wallet.

The daughter began the conversation by softening the issue with humor. Moreover, there was clear indication that her need for money was not for illegitimate reasons, but for practical, necessary reasons. That is a slight manipulation. A father will feel a tinge of guilt in questioning a child's needs and finding the purpose is entirely sane. His daughter now has a leg up. When her father asks if her boyfriend is taking advantage of her, his daughter turns the tables and, in fact, suggests her parents are using her to run her sister to practices and not covering her gas costs. The guilt level increases. Her father ends up paying her more than she requested – partly out of love and obligation to her needs – but in large part based on guilt. He was manipulated.

Advertisers are the most adept at manipulation, even if they are not cognizant of their underlying methods. I was not aware dandruff was a social crime until I began seeing "Head and Shoulders" advertisements. The ads created the problem; and dandruff became a social calamity. The advertisers drove fear levels up, and then provided the remedy – the control. A decade later, feminine hygiene became the alarming concern. Smart advertisers created fear of feminine odor, then provided the means of control, through purchase of an unneeded product.

Manipulation is part of the dance of humanity. It is not necessarily bad; it just is. And manipulation, from the baby's cry to the daughter's request for money, is about gaining control. Those who are able to manipulate others feel reduced fear; they feel they can control their environments. For those whose attempts at manipulation have traditionally been unsuccessful, fear and anxiety elevate. And when fear and anxiety increase, the need to over-control occurs.

ALIENS

Several years ago, a friend of mine administered a psychiatric evaluation to a patient, as part of a request from a State agency. The patient, in his late thirties, had a diagnosis of schizophrenia. He had been plagued with fears of being abducted by aliens whom, he explained, on multiple occasions had strapped him down nude in a sterile room on board their ship and taken blood, probed him, run scans and then released him. He was sure he was being tracked through devices implanted in his brain and would be abducted again.

The psychologist decided to try something unconventional and have x-rays taken, as a means of potentially helping the patient with resetting his cognitive position. The patient agreed. A day later, the psychologist sat across from the patient. "I'm not sure how to tell you this, he began, but there has been a peculiar finding." The patient nodded, interested.

"The x-rays reveal there are what appear to be two metal implants in your forehead." He showed him the x-ray. The patient, again, nodded.

"Was there perhaps an accident in your past you didn't tell me about?"

"No," the patient answered. "Did you find anything else?"

The doctor pondered, uncomfortable. "No. But I can't explain this."

"Oh, I can," he said. "I put two needles under the skin in my forehead."

The doctor sat back. "Why?"

"I just wanted to be sure the x-rays you showed me were mine."

CHAPTER FIFTEEN

EMOTIONAL DISORDERS

To be ill adjusted to a deranged world is not a breakdown.

-Jeanette Winterson

A child's world is his parents. If parents respond to needs, the child gains confidence he has the ability to control his world. Parents who respond to a child's needs suggest the individual is protected and that the world will take care of him.

The child grows up with a base of confidence, faith and safety net. His fear level is, thus, eased.

A child whose guardians do not respond to his needs is raised to believe he has no control and there is no safety net. The message is the child is not protected and the world will not take care of him. Faith does not develop – be it religious or otherwise. The child, and later the adult, is scared to death. He overcompensates for his lack of control, faith and confidence. His immense fear translates into over-control, and the fear morphs into jealousy, anger and rage.

The Diagnostic and Statistical Manual of Mental Disorders (Fifth Edition), the tool used almost exclusively for diagnosing mental disorders, breaks psychiatric conditions into several general categories and conditions. For many conditions, bio-chemistry may be responsible for clusters of symptoms and behaviors, but the foundational fear and need for control remains the filter between the unconscious and consciousness, and it is fear that is responsible for aberrant behavior.

According to a report by the National Institutes of Health, "Fear is the emotion that has been most successfully studied. Fear is required for our survival, but when it is not regulated, it becomes responsible for anxiety disorders and some of the symptoms of depression."

Anxiety Disorders include panic attacks, specific phobias, separation anxiety disorder, selective mutism, social phobias, agoraphobia (fear of being in public places) and generalized anxiety disorder. Anxiety Disorders, according the DSM-5, are due to excessive fear and anxiety. The foundation for these disorders is fear (ultimately of death) and loss of control.

Gambling is an obsessive-compulsive behavior. Gambling is about emotionally attempting to control that which, intellectually, we recognize we cannot. The intent is to gain control (usually money) through behavioral efforts, by trying over and over again. Casinos rely on control drive for their cash cow. Video games and electronic phone games also sit on the obsessive-compulsive drive to control, and players set internal goals or faux goals – if I win I am the ruler of the world…of my family…in my relationship…of happiness.

Panic Disorder and panic attacks bring symptoms of sweating, trembling, heart palpitations, numbness, chest discomfort and feelings of choking. Two additional symptoms listed in the diagnostic manual are "fear of losing control" and "fear of dying." While panic attacks may present in individuals more biologically susceptible, the underlying cause, without regard to the bio-chemistry sitting atop the foundational reason, is breakdown of the defense mechanisms which are suppressing the fear of death. Often, the onset of panic attacks follows an incident, wherein denial of mortality was difficult to protect. A panic attack may occur following a traumatic event, such as a car accident or a medical emergency. Panic attacks may also begin following trauma experienced by somebody close to you. The panic is associated with the realization of the fragility of life, and the defense mechanism becomes weakened. Post-traumatic stress disorder is long term suppression of the defense mechanisms protecting us from conscious awareness of our mortality.

John was 65 years old when he had his first heart attack. He had been retired only one month from a high stress position in the steel industry. He and his wife had saved well, and he had the added insurance of a company retirement. Financially, they were in a good place, which enabled them to sell their home and move to a home on the ocean, purchase a 34 foot fishing boat and consider traveling the world.

A late night trip to the ER three months after John retired revealed ninety percent occlusion in a cardiac artery. John required emergency by-pass surgery. It was surreal. He had spent nearly 40 years working in the thick of a high pressure industry, and on the threshold of the life he had always imagined, he was facing life threatening medical conditions.

There is no way to know if retirement had anything to do with John's medical situation. It would seem implausible that his heart disease was connected with work cessation. However, in a wide-sweeping review of 22 longitudinal studies of the health effects of retirement, reported in BMC Public Health in 2013, there was strong evidence physical health declined following retirement, as compared with those who continued working. John had just moved from an Executive VP position in a major U.S. company, a position in which he was highly regarded and respected, to not knowing exactly what to expect day to day. In his work role, he was the lightening rod for talent acquisition and retention, for closing down plants and leading the way into the next century and generation of the corporation. When John retired, he lost substantial control. One day in June, thousands of employees looked to him for leadership; the next day he was moving to a part of the country with which he was unfamiliar, purchasing a boat he knew he wasn't adept at piloting and considering taking up golf, which had never really appealed to him before.

Almost immediately following his bypass surgery, John began having panic attacks. He would wake up sweating, and his heart would palpitate. Each trip to emergency revealed no physical explanation. As he moved farther into retirement and away from the post-op, the panic attacks dissipated. However, the panic attacks returned twice, just prior to leaving for separate trips to Europe.

Panic Disorder may trickle into other anxiety disorders. Agoraphobia sometimes develops in conjunction with panic attacks, wherein individuals are fearful of leaving home, because the fear of being trapped in a panic state or fear of losing control in public. Selective mutism, a failure to speak in specific social situations, elicits the dichotomy of losing control and over-controlling; individuals' fear of speaking in social situations is typically based in fear of embarrassment, of being socially out of control, but the mutism is selective, meaning the individual is taking control and not speaking.

Obsessive-Compulsive Disorders are characterized by recurrent, persistent thoughts, urges and behaviors aimed at reducing or preventing anxiety. Patients believe if they do not perform compulsive rituals, cataclysm will occur, including the patient's death or the death of loved ones. OCD is manifested in an individual's fear of losing control and, through the ritualistic behavior, there is belief the catastrophe will be averted. The "step on the crack, break your mother's back," rhyme is a description of the quandary a person with OCD faces.

I worked with a 14 year old boy who was late for school nearly every day, because he was lining up all his toy soldiers on his desk in a very specific way before he left each morning. He was convinced if the soldiers were not perfectly placed, something horrible would happen to his mother while he was gone. While he intellectually understood the absurdity of his thoughts and behaviors, he couldn't leave for school unless the soldiers were perfectly situated. This child's OCD was rooted in his fear of losing all control and attempting, through a ritualistic process, to gain control. As is the case with almost all cases of OCD, the patient was aware the underlying fear was about death.

"Hit and Run" OCD manifests in patients' fears they have run over and killed a pedestrian while driving. Renee's onset of her OCD came in early adulthood, after she had given birth to her first child. The disorder was debilitating. She obsessed continuously about running over a child or adult, thus she compulsively looked into her mirror to see if she had hit someone. Often she circled back to see whom she had killed. At the height of her symptoms, she experienced great difficulty reaching her destination, namely work, which caused obvious problems.

Renee's symptoms were rooted in her fear of losing control, resulting in death. When Renee was 6 years old her father was killed in an automobile accident. Her symptoms, however, did not begin until she was 27. For years she was able to suppress her fears, but the birth of her daughter, and the responsibility she had for protecting her daughter's life, was overwhelming. Her doubts about her ability to control her world and protect her daughter came crashing through.

Post-Traumatic Stress Disorder has been at the front of the media the last several years, not surprisingly, given the decade-long conflict in the Middle East. While there are many factors involved in PTSD, the underlying issue is the sense of loss of control and the loss of control leading to death. In PTSD, the defense mechanism (denial of mortality) has been damaged. Individuals who develop PTSD have typically been in a life threatening situation, such as combat, an automobile accident or, far too commonly, child sexual abuse or neglect. The illusion of control is stripped away, and the fear of death comes bounding through. The person with PTSD knows control is an illusion and fear, which had been suppressed, hemorrhages through.

I worked with a police officer several years ago who had been called to a domestic disturbance. A husband was holding hostage his wife and refused to come out of the house. The officer, a twenty-two year veteran, went around the rear of the house and gained entry at the back door. The door led to a landing area that opened to stairs going to the basement and a step up into the kitchen. He closed the door behind himself to cover his entry, and he immediately came under fire. The perpetrator expended two rapid shotgun rounds into the wall, blowing large chunks of wood and plaster onto the officer. He reloaded before the officer could get a shot off, and over the next hour kept him pinned on the stairwell.

Officer Sheen had never fired his weapon in the line of duty. He had no reference for the terror he felt. While other officers tried to talk the man into surrendering, they knew the prognosis was bad. Sheen was paralyzed with fear, and only after an hour's time, when police distracted the perpetrator, was Sheen able to move. He shot and killed the man who had fired at him, but he would never pick up his service pistol again. The 22 year police veteran, who had never done anything but police work, was finished. His sense of control was gone. He took a disability severance 8 months later.

The mind is such a powerful and mysterious entity. It maintains an array of tools to protect the ego and bolster resolve. Defense mechanisms like denial, projection and reaction formation are common and tend to protect people from everyday emotional assaults. The mind must build walls of protection to ward off complete destruction of the ego. Dissociative Identity Disorder, often referred to as Multiple Personality Disorder, occurs rarely but when it does it is most often found in the aftermath of early and sustained childhood trauma, most commonly sexual trauma. In DID, the individual builds separate and distinct personality states to protect against assaults and traumatic scars.

DID is an amazing example of the mind's potential to protect. In multiple personality disorder, some personalities are left-handed, while the core personality is right-handed. There are voice alterations, dialectical changes, paralyses, visual acuity differences, cat and medication allergies and changes on EEG scans and brain blood flow.

DID is about control. The abuse sustained in those diagnosed with DID would be more accurately described as torture. When abuse is so significant and overwhelming, victims self-hypnotize to escape.

In a study of murderers on death row, a disproportionate number were diagnosed with DID. It should be noted none of the prisoners in the study used DID as a legal defense, and the core personality rarely had memory of any abuse. Most of the abuse was documented and verified by family members or social departments.

The documents verifying childhood trauma of the prisoners were exceptionally disturbing. One of the murderers diagnosed with DID was dressed up like a girl by his grandmother and given to his grandfather for sex. Another had been used by a stepfather to make pornographic films. One inmate had no recollection of his ongoing incestuous relationship with his mother. Another inmate had been deliberately set afire by his parents, and another had scars on his buttocks from having been made to sit repeatedly on a red hot stove.

Individuals develop DID in childhood to escape the trauma being inflicted upon them. The terror these individuals experienced was so great, escape was essential. Individuals who dissociate are also often able to self-anesthetize to mitigate pain. They control their worlds by creating alter-worlds. During traumatic events, individuals with DID self-hypnotize and transport themselves into a different personality, becoming someone other than the victim. They push down the fear of death by escaping the situation entirely. In doing so, they also maintain the illusion of having control, by burying memories of being out of control. Further, they fabricate memories, imagining their caretakers as supportive and nurturing.

Of eating disorders, anorexia nervosa (AN), bulimia and binge-eating are the most recognizable. The core issue in eating disorders is fear and control. Individuals with anorexia fear getting fat. They develop disturbances in body perception (believing they are overweight) and, thereby, reduce food intake. The fear of gaining weight is really about fear of losing control, and the ultimate fear of loss of control is death. Binge eating is uncontrolled eating. Underlying is an "acute feeling of loss of control." The individual then controls the outcome by self induced vomiting (controlling by losing control), laxatives and other medications.

There is a great deal of controversy about the underlying causes for AN. Some studies concluded there was higher incidence of childhood sexual trauma, but it appears the incidence is no higher than in the general population. What stand out are the obsessive-compulsive tendencies of those who develop NA. Persons with eating disorders are more likely to expect perfection in grades, performance and achievement. The common thread is the need to control, fear of loss of control being the fundamental concern.

Anxiety, a more generalized, inarticulate fear, often runs co-morbidly with depression. Depression occurs when hope dissipates. Hope is built on ability to control. Hopelessness is the perceived absence of control. Individuals who are depressed feel little to no control in their lives.

Situational depression, as opposed to a more enduring, biochemical depression, tends to come with enormous loss. Grieving a death or the loss of a relationship can bring depression. Depressed people present a sad affect. Sometimes there are bursts of anger, as anger sits on fear. Depressed individuals may not want to get out of bed, take showers or perform any function. They have, at some level, given up being in control.

I worked with a young woman several years ago who presented as clinically depressed. She was attending college and still living at home with her mother and father. Because she was still dependent, her father did not give her the autonomy she believed she deserved. He maintained a curfew for her, indicated the friends with whom he thought she should hang out and regulated who she dated. She believed she needed to pursue her educational goals, and she could not find work that would provide her income enough for her to move out and attend school. She felt trapped. We explored the control issues with her father. Bringing the issues to the level of consciousness enabled her to determine what she thought she could control and what she could live with. Much of her depression abated. In a psychological study performed in 2009, it was revealed individuals who believe their lives were controlled by chance had significantly higher levels of depression than did individuals who believed they asserted control over their lives.

Psychotic disorders, such as schizophrenia, can be debilitating. While the symptoms of disorders like schizophrenia almost certainly spring from bio-chemical origins, the ways in which psychosis manifests offers a window into foundations of control. The person with obsessive-compulsive disorder intellectually knows her OCD is irrational. The person with schizophrenia, when in the throes of psychosis, does not maintain such conscious perspective. A psychotic episode, by definition, is being out of touch with reality. The person with psychosis truly believes the hallucinations and delusions are real.

When the drape of defense is stripped away by psychotic disorders, we can see the fear operating in the unconscious. Delusions, or beliefs not based in reality, and hallucinations, visual and auditory, frame psychotic disorders. Delusions are broken down into types. Persecutory delusions are unfounded beliefs a person is going to be harmed by someone or some group. The delusion is fear. Grandiose delusions, on the other hand, are about individuals possessing grand powers. In the grandiose state individuals believe they cannot be harmed. The delusion is control. A man diagnosed with schizophrenia with grandiose delusions was quoted: "I am God; I created the universe and I am son of Prince Phillip. I am also a famous DJ. I have superman-type powers."

Persons with nihilistic delusions believe a major catastrophe is going to occur. These delusions are, of course, about impending doom, death and loss of control. Somatic delusions focus on health concerns, including delusions of terminal illness and loss of bodily control. In a report on a pregnant woman diagnosed with nihilistic and somatic delusions, the physician reported, "The patient complained that her liver was "putrefying" and her heart was "altogether absent.""

Mental illness is the breakdown of defenses protecting against fear of death. Thus, all mental health issues, from general anxiety to full blown psychosis, are rooted in fear of loss of control and delusions of grand control.

The DSM-V rarely mentions the word control and does not attribute, overtly at least, psychiatric conditions to fear of loss of control and the drive to control. The reality, however, is all psychiatric conditions are fueled by fear and the need to mitigate the fear through control.

A Poem I Wrote About Asperger's ~ Secret Soul

"Inwardly sensitive
Outwardly dead
No one sees the real me
She's trapped inside my head

Explaining her through words
One could never comprehend
Distortion occurs from my brain to my lips

Utterances I can't muster flow out into script
Left for those without insight to misinterpret
Inside to outside to inside again
Words flow through my soul to be cast to the wind

My mind is my freedom
All the same my prison
Is it pure hell or an oasis I live in?
I wish someone could break through to my dimension

Solitude, alone, aloof, loner: Division
Freak, outcast, smart-ass: Exclusion

BONES IN A BOX

Words come and go

Words ebb and flow

Words cold as ice

Words hot as smoke

Some words are full of wisdom

Some words you let go

I'll find my words someday

When I do the world will know

Until then…

Inwardly sensitive

Outwardly dead

Just another soul locked inside her head"

CHAPTER SIXTEEN

AUTISM

Some days I just want to climb inside my own skin and hide.

-TinaJ. Richardson

There is no typical day at the Burger School for Students with Autism. Over 300 individuals, aged from pre-school to 26, from the largest county in Michigan attend, vying to improve social, academic and practical living skills.

Screams and self-abusive behavior, aggression and OCD manifestations are common at Burger. Some students walk the halls to release tension; others are practicing social and business acumen by selling coffee and cookies from classroom to classroom. Students work in the woodshop, building the set for the upcoming musical production, and others rock in front of computers, using technology as a learning tool, grunting or laughing when receiving feedback for correct answers. Observing students striking out at staff with clenched fists or throwing a chair across the room is not uncommon. Nor is it uncommon to witness a student with autism approach with a friendly, practiced self-introduction, applying the training obtained at the school. Intellectual levels vary for individuals on the autism spectrum as much as they do with people in the general population, and students' personalities are varied, as well; there are more differences than likenesses in these students, but some behaviors typify autism. The vacant stare, the awkwardness of communication and intonation are thematic.

Social communication and social interaction is always a challenge in the world of autism. Eye contact and reading nonverbal cues tend, in some ways, to define autism, as do challenges with integrated verbal skills and establishing and maintaining relationships. In reports by parents of children with autism, there are usually similarities noted in their kids in pre-school. Children later diagnosed with autism were reported to be slow in obtaining, or nearly absent in development of, expressive language skills. They often are described as sitting alone in groups of same aged peers, staring off into space or fixated on moving, rotating objects. Some parents noted hand flapping and rocking and peculiar obsessions with objects or ideas. A student may compulsively build paper airplanes and save boxes of them in the closet or under the bed, raging when parents suggest cleaning them out. A child may flap his hands when excited, walk toe to heel and have no interest in other children or people. His verbal utterances may be limited to repeating phrases over and over, or grunting or squealing. Individuals with autism often report being over-stimulated, to the extent they cover their ears to block out the noise. Sometimes they want to be squeezed or held tightly to suppress the sensitivities felt from scratchy clothing and others' touches.

When those of us without autism become frightened, overwhelmingly frightened, our language centers essentially shut down. We are, as noted earlier, rendered speechless. Our brains switch into survival mode, into our animal brains. Clinicians working with patients with post-traumatic stress disorder have known for some time that talk therapy doesn't really work. In recent years, PET Scans have revealed why; language centers cease operation when the brain is processing trauma and readying for fight or flight. Trauma and fear engage the limbic system, the part of the brain that doesn't reason and plan but reacts and tries to survive. Memories of traumatic events, therefore, cannot typically be accessed through language, because the trauma was never stored there. Research on individuals who suffered abuse and trauma, when corrected for other factors, reveals language acquisition can be permanently damaged.

Those with autism are nearly always overwhelmed over a lifetime. When the brain is bombarded by feelings of fear and trauma, language becomes inaccessible. Recent brain imaging studies reveal, in many individuals with autism, that when auditory stimuli is presented, the auditory receptor area of the brain shuts down, and the right side, the non-auditory side, takes over. So, the brain trains itself to suppress incoming stimulation, potentially because it is too overwhelming. The result is that auditory stimulation is blocked out and language storage and retrieval are shut down.

Aggression, biting, rocking and screaming are not uncommon behaviors in persons with autism. Aggression, biting, rocking and screaming are also associated with individuals terrorized and attempting to control their worlds. Fear begets the need to control, and in autism these components of fear and controlling behavior are clearly evident.

Flapping is a hallmark motoric behavior in autism. But hand flapping is also seen in developmentally typical children when emotions are heightened. Fear is always at the base of emotion, so hand flapping is linked inextricably to fear. Flapping movements increase in frequency when a child is stressed or anxious. Adults also may flap their hands when frightened. One individual noted that as an adult she "flapped (her) right hand like mad while choking." While hand flapping is something of a signature behavior in individuals with autism, it can also be clearly linked to typical individuals when they are very frightened and emotional.

Obsessive-compulsive behaviors are also one of the hallmarks of autism. In the non-autism population, OCD is linked with anxiety and percolating fear. Freud talked about obsessions and compulsions as a means of "binding" anxiety. Obsessive thinking is generally fueled by fear – something bad will happen if you don't engage in the compulsive behavior. The boy who lined up his soldiers feared his mother would die if the compulsion was not carried out.

Recent research by the National Institute of Mental Health reveals the amygdalae (the fear centers) in people with autism are initially abnormally large. Over time, the hyperactivity in the amygdala causes the brain to compensate, killing amygdala cells and causing the structure to shrink and become abnormally underactive. The fear centers in the brain of individuals with autism, thus, appear to be overactive at the stage in life when the brain is being wired for language, fear response and reading social cues from others. Due to the over-activity of the fear center, language acquisition is suppressed, and auditory processing is rerouted. The wiring of the brain, due to the over-active amygdala, is altered. The amygdala runs hot, like an accelerator stuck wide open; the brain compensates and shuts it down. The result is a brain wired to circumvent the language center and reconfigure the way auditory information is routed. Then, after the amygdala shrinks, recognition of social cues and reading of facial expression diminishes. (We read fear in others through eye contact and empathy, both skills of which are significantly impaired in those with autism.)

There have been many theories associated with the causes of autism; I am not suggesting knowledge of cause, nor am I offering a different approach to the treatment for autism. I am strongly suggesting, however, that autism is rooted in fear and need to control. While research seems to support the fear center is a significant component of autism, I further suggest autism is, in some way, rooted in alteration to the fear center.

I Am – I Will – I Live – I Fly

A dozen pairs of eyes were staring her way. The only thing between her and complete nakedness was a thin robe. And she was about to drop the robe, step upon a platform, and stand before all of these people without a stitch of clothing. The instructor looked at her, letting her know the time had come. She took a deep breath and let the robe fall to the floor. She'd never felt so exposed, so vulnerable. After a few minutes of staring over the heads of everyone in the room, she dared a skittish glance. They were intently focused on sketching her, their faces composed in concentration. She didn't feel judged. They were viewing her body as the human form. She was art. She began to relax. Over the next hour, she not only felt confident standing naked before these artists — she felt empowered. Not so much because she was showing off her body, but because she dared to do something she feared so deeply. If she could do this, she could do anything. Imagine that feeling — having the self confidence to fearlessly do anything you set your mind to. Imagine being able to drop your metaphorical robe and master the thing that scares you. Most confident people weren't born that way. Like everyone, they've had their share of fears and insecurities. But confident people haven't allowed fears and insecurities to control their destinies. They've learned to be proactive in changing the thoughts, behaviors, and decisions that keep them stuck in a compromised and contained life.

CHAPTER SEVENTEEN

CONFIDENCE

All you need in this life is ignorance and confidence, and then success is sure.

-Mark Twain

Truly I say to you, if you have faith and do not doubt, you will not only do what was done to the fig tree, but even if you say to this mountain, 'Be taken up and cast into the sea,' it will happen.

-Jesus

Confidence is the face of self-control, past success, faith and knowledge. Confidence projects control – and that is why we are drawn to confidence. Confidence suggests deep understanding and wisdom. It calms, because there is a sense the individual with confidence understands and predicts the environment and others more adroitly. Hollywood in the 1940s and 1950s understood, at some level, the importance of confidence; Cary Grant, Frank Sinatra, Sidney Portier, Humphrey Bogart and Loren Bacall exuded confidence and people wanted to see them, to be around them.

In a study of more than 500 students, academics and workers reported in The Journal of Personality and Social Psychology those who appeared more confident achieved a higher social status than their peers. Attraction to confidence is predictable, given unconscious need to be in control. Self-confident people are more successful in all areas of life, and people are drawn to those with confidence.

Cockiness and narcissism are not the same as confidence, though people can be fooled. Individuals with narcissistic personality disorder or other personality disorders often present a shell of confidence, but when the ego of such a person is threatened they over-control. Sociopaths don't have a conscience, so the shell of confidence is a conscious act, an observed and practiced recitation. Unfortunately, there are many individuals in politics and at the helm of large companies who do, in fact, fool people.

Consider a person you believe to be highly confident. I bet the person speaks evenly and calmly. The confident person is predictable, sets safe boundaries, is logical and has expectations of success. Others trust confident people and, as such, confident people have more friends, reach higher levels of work success and become leaders.

Mark Leary, a noted self-esteem researcher at Wake Forest University, indicates a confident person looks relaxed, calm and poised. Self-confident people tend to stand taller with their heads up. They engage in more direct eye contact. He further observed that our "primate cousins" reveal the same. "Chimps and gorillas with power--the strongest ones--convey this in their body language." Audrey Brodt, a Denver psychologist and business consultant observes, "A giveaway for people who want to look confident but they aren't is that they talk too much." The need to fill voids of silence with chatter is a measure of over-control.

Legendary Stanford University psychologist Albert Bandura indicated peoples' beliefs in their abilities determine the outcomes. People who believe they can, work harder and are less deterred than those with low levels of confidence. "Confident people approach threatening situations with assurances that they can exercise control."

Leary points out that when failure occurs, confident people heighten and sustain their efforts. They recover their sense of confidence after failures or setbacks. They attribute failure to insufficient effort or a lack of knowledge and skills that are attainable. In other words, they believe they are in control, and if they haven't achieved a goal it is because enough effort wasn't put in.

True confidence is based in faith. That faith can be religious, but it can also be founded on family roots of wealth and privilege. Confidence requires something deeper, a belief system that is based in a more fundamental sense of mission. Confident people believe they can get it done. It is this belief, not the hope, which provides foundation for the long, hard fight. If you think you can you have a shot; if you believe you can't, you can't.

Confidence is the projection of perceived sense of control. An individual's confidence is based in faith he has control. Regardless of circumstances, there is the sense things will work out. It is a belief the outcome sought will be attained. Belief is the underpinning of confidence, and belief is promoted by past success and historic entitlement. A man who believes in himself or some deeper spiritual base, is typically calm, thoughtful and predictable in the face of adversity. Confidence is an aura, a crown of sorts, a badge signifying control.

Consider the following individuals:

Liam Neeson George Clooney Jeff Bridges

Bruce Springsteen	Diane Sawyer	Stephen King
Gwenyth Paltrow	Bill Clinton	Ronald Reagan
Paul Newman	Dalai Llama	Oprah
Steve McQueen	Russell Crowe	Barack Obama
George H. Bush	Shaquille O'Neal	

Now note whether, in your opinion, each is:

intelligent vs. sub-average

stoic vs. overbearing

strong vs. weak

well-spoken vs. inarticulate

creative vs. stuck

self-reliant vs. dependent

thoughtful vs. wreckless

wise vs. short-sighted

The point is, the compiled list of names include individuals who are often viewed as intelligent, strong, well-spoken, creative, self-reliant, thoughtful and wise. These are also the qualities that describe individuals considered to be confident. We are drawn to such people. We trust such people.

However, when fear deepens, or when individuals, political or otherwise, manipulate fear, society overlooks the need for pensive, thoughtful wisdom and grabs the coattails of those who are loudest and most threatening. We mistake bravado with confidence. The person who thunders threats of violence toward terrorist organizations temporarily quells the fear, and we as a society stop thinking with our frontal lobes and react to our limbic systems, our fear centers.

Understanding fear and our need to control is essential to our human survival. Fear has caused tragic social reaction in the past and will undoubtedly cause such reaction in the future.

CHAPTER EIGHTEEN

MONEY

While money can't buy happiness, it certainly lets you choose your own form of misery.

-Groucho Marx

Money controls. Money is a tool for acquisition of control. Those who have the most money control the most. Those with the least control little.

The first forms of money, not including bartering, were food sources. Livestock was used as a monetary form from 9000 BC to 6000 BC. Later, agricultural resources were used. So, at the root of money is sustenance, without which life cannot continue.

As with pure control, money abates fear. When money problems increase, fear increases. The fear is not based on the absence of dollar bills; it is predicated on not having what money buys – namely survival. The nearer we come to not having the bartering power of money, the more anxious we become.

In the past 10 years, over $32 billion has been spent on lobbying political leaders. The money, thus, converts to controlling national policy and legislation. The money spent is essentially an investment, typically yielding opportunity to make more money to influence more control over the political machine.

Jane Mayer, in the August 2010 Issue of the New Yorker, writes about philanthropist David H. Koch. Koch has donated a hundred million dollars to modernize the Lincoln Center's New York State Theatre, twenty million to the American Museum of Natural History, ten million dollars to renovate the Metropolitan Museum of Art and forty million dollars to the Sloan-Kettering Cancer Center.

Koch Industries, which has annual revenues estimated at over 100 billion dollars and is ranked by Forbes as the second-largest private company in the United States, puts David and Charles Koch behind only Bill Gates and Warren Buffett in fortune. The Koch brothers, in addition to owning Brawny paper towels, Dixie cup, Georgia-Pacific lumber and

Stainmaster Carpet operate oil refineries in Alaska, Texas and Minnesota. As such, many of the donations made by Koch Industries have more insidious purpose.

According to the University of Massachusetts at Amherst's Political Economy Research Institute, Koch Industries is also one of the top ten air polluters in the United States. A Greenpeace report stated Koch Industries was a "kingpin of climate science denial," and between 2005 and 2008 gave more money than Exxon Mobil in fighting legislation related to climate change. David Koch is also credited with starting the organization Americans for Prosperity Foundation. The foundation has been directly connected with training Tea Party activists in Texas. David Axelrod, Obama's senior adviser, said, "What they don't say is that, in part, this (The Tea Party) is a grassroots citizens' movement brought to you by a bunch of oil billionaires." A Republican campaign consultant who has done research on behalf of Charles and David Koch said of the Tea Party, "The Koch brothers gave the money that founded it. It's like they put the seeds in the ground. Then the rainstorm comes, and the frogs come out of the mud—and they're our candidates!" The Kochs provided the funding for the first libertarian think tank, the Cato Institute, which took out a full page advertisement in the Times contradicting Obama's admonishment that global warming science is beyond dispute.

Cato "scholars" have been coined the "Climategate" conspiracy.

Money is a tool used to obtain control, but politics is another level; politics is controlling directly, and when money and the control money can buy is bled out, direct control is the natural next step. Politics is not so much about serving the public as gaining and asserting more control. Thirty three of the forty seven United States Presidents have been millionaires. That equates to 68%, compared with 2% in the general population. Twenty two presidents (45%) were worth over 10 million. And about 15% had wealth exceeding $100 million. George Washington's wealth in today's dollars was over half a billion. It is almost counter-intuitive to believe men who have amassed such huge fortunes maintain deep objectives in serving others. Money is about control. Political control is about power and manipulation.

Michael Bloomberg, the three-time New York City Mayor, had enough money to do anything he wanted. He is by most accounts the 8th wealthiest person in the United States and the 13th wealthiest in the world. He could sail with family and friends on the sleekest yachts, in the most beautiful places in the world. His net worth is $36.5 billion. Billion. And Mr. Bloomberg, who had undoubtedly clawed his way to the top of the wealth-heap determined he wanted to be in charge of one of the most dynamic cities on Earth.

Huge fortunes do not guarantee a place in the White House, but many with great wealth have attempted to reach the Oval Office. Some of the more modern candidates include Steve Forbes, Ross Perot, Mitt Romney, John Kerry, Ted Kennedy, Al Gore and Nelson Rockefeller. All had fortunes exceeding $100 million. I may be jaded, but it seems unlikely the motivation for seeking office for most of these individuals on the above list was purely serving the good of the country.

Congress, the group representing the interests of all of us, consists of 245 millionaires. Approximately 66% of the Senate and 41% of the House are millionaires. While being a millionaire is not inherently negative, using public office as a means for controlling outcomes and enhancing personal holdings is at best a conflict of interest and worse a high-jacking of liberty.

Money buys power, and power is the control that lords over systems and large groups of people. Power is control exacerbated, and individuals seeking power are no longer looking for the illusion of control by way of movies and sports; they are living the illusion of control. Power can, thus, be very dangerous; the danger is underscored by recent support for presidential candidates who use fear to set the stage and aggressive rhetoric as means of appearing to be in control.

FAMILY GUY – MAYORAL DEBATE

Man: Mayor West, if you are reelected, would you increase the frequency of garbage pick-up?

Mayor: Sir, that's an excellent question, and I thank you for it. I think it's great we live in a town where you can ask questions, because without questions we just have answers. And an answer without a question is a statement.

Man: Oh, I like him. He looks me in the eye.

Another man: I'd like to have a beer with him. I'm voting for him.

Lois to Brian: I don't understand these people. He didn't even say anything and they're eatin' it up.

Brian the Dog: Lois, undecided voters are the biggest idiots on the planet. Try giving short, simple answers.

Moderator to Another Man: Sir, your question please?

Audience Participant: Mrs. Griffin, what do you plan to do about crime in our city?

Lois: (Thinking) A lot.

RAVING APPLAUSE

Lois continues…Because that's what Jesus wants.

LOUDER APPLAUSE

Lois, now confident: 911 was bad!

APPLAUSE ESCALATES

Audience participant: I agree with that.

Lois: I can't believe how easy this is.

Man: Mrs. Griffin, what are your plans about cleaning up our environment?

Lois (thoughtful): 911!

RAUCOUS CLAPPING

Woman: Mrs Griffin, what about our traffic problem?

Lois: Nine…(expectant gasp from audience) …Eleven!

CHAPTER NINETEEN

LEADERS

Suppose you were an idiot, and suppose you were a member of Congress; but I repeat myself.

-Mark Twain

Control is not merely an academic concern. Leaders, by definition, assume control. Therefore, the makeup of a leader, as reflection of the leader's psyche, history and developmental dynamics, is critical to us all. Many variables push people into leadership roles. It is imperative we know why an individual wants to lead. This is an area that gets so little attention, yet the psychological and family history of a leader is grandly important to all of us.

Leaders who do not believe there is a greater control, who believe all control must come from them, are most dangerous. A man who is controlling as overcompensation for internal terrors can bring cataclysmic events on society. Leaders with strong faith will tend not to over-control. These leaders believe there is already a positive control in place. When I speak of faith I am not suggesting a specific religion or belief; there are a number of ways to develop spiritual and/or faith based beliefs.

Many great leaders come from privileged backgrounds. Privilege itself provides sense of control and immortality. If you come from a line of British aristocracy, you are more likely to believe in your own immortality than a person who has skittered between homelessness and oppressive landlord living. Descendents of aristocracy see the solid line of ancestry as consistent privilege. There is control at the foundation - a safety net. Privilege also brings money, which is itself a tool of control.

Winston Churchill led Great Britain through WWII, when Adolph Hitler was avariciously reaching across Europe, invading and occupying nations. The Nazis hammered England with raids by air, and despite the fact England sustained more mortar fire than any other European country, under Churchill's leadership, the nation survived the war.

Churchill was from a line aristocracy. His father was a duke and had expectation Churchill would continue the family nobility. Churchill and his father were not particularly close, though Churchill had a tight relationship with his mother. When his father insisted Churchill attend a top European preparatory school, Churchill was forced to move away from his mother and the security she provided. When Churchill was 18 his father died. The timing of his father's death may have unconsciously catapulted him into a leadership role.

Churchill's aristocracy is foundation for confidence and control. He came from a long line of powerful people. His family had wealth. His education was deluxe. In his darkest hours he recognized, at some level, his family legacy of leadership and foundation. Winston Churchill's deep faith in family roots provided him the expectation of success. He did not acquiesce to fear, because he believed there was a larger, positive control.

Franklin Delano Roosevelt was also raised in wealth and privilege. FDR, initially tutored at home, attended a series of exclusive schools, graduating from Harvard and attending Columbia Law School. Roosevelt was related to Theodore Roosevelt, the 36th U.S. President, and his mother was a wealthy socialite. His mother was strong and was intent on Roosevelt not being spoiled. The combination of privilege and hard work replicated, in some ways, Churchill's experiences.

As a very young adult, Roosevelt contracted Polio and, thus, endured more personal challenge. FDR's father died, similarly to Churchill's, when Franklin was 20.

John F. Kennedy also came from a line of privilege and wealth. His father, with whom Kennedy had a strained relationship, was a United States Ambassador and Statesman. As with FDR and Churchill, Kennedy attended the most prestigious schools. He also dealt with a plethora of personal challenges with his health, as a child. As a very young adult, Kennedy's brother, Joe, whom their father hoped would be president, was killed in the war. Kennedy's faith in his blood line, wealth, religious base and his own abilities helped him overcome adversity. His confidence and belief he was in control mitigated knee jerk reactions to fear.

Adolf Hitler, on the other hand, was never sure of his lineage. His grandfather did not know who his father was, he having been born to an unmarried servant girl working for a Jewish businessman. There has been speculation Hitler's great-grandfather was Jewish. Hitler's father was impoverished, illegitimate and was given up for adoption by his mother when he was five.

Lack of knowledge of foundation leaves no foundation. There is no sense of foundational control, because there are no roots. Adoptive children are two times more likely to be clinically depressed, attempt suicide and successfully complete suicide when all other variables are adjusted for. While most adoptive children adjust well, the statistics are telling. The lack of felt control often results in need for over-control, and depression and violent acquisition of control are indicators of perceived lack of control. It is frightening to not know one's foundation, and that lack of knowledge puts some at greater risk.

Adolph Hitler's father, Alois Hitler, was controlling and abusive. Adolph's sister, Paula Hitler, reported Adolph was beaten by their father every day. Hitler described to others how he resolved not to make a sound when his father beat him. Once he reported, without emotion, to his mother, 'Father hit me thirty-two times.'

His mother's weakness, with regard to interceding on Adolf''s behalf, was another foundational weakness in Hitler's life. When his mother, Klara, was sixteen she moved in with her Uncle Alois, to care for his dying wife and two children. Alois impregnated her; he was forty-eight and she twenty-four. Within two and a half years Klara gave birth to three children. Diphtheria hit the home, and a few weeks after giving birth to her third child, all three of the children were dead. In the same year she again became pregnant, and in April of the following year gave birth to Adolph.

It is impossible to fully understand the psychological dynamics she was struggling with. However, it is known

Adolph's father felt substantial lack of control in who he was. He had little confidence, so he over-controlled, much of that manifesting in beatings of Adolph. His mother was devastated by her loss, so she certainly would have felt no control. She lived with a controlling man, and fear of death ruled her life. She had lost three children and unconsciously feared losing Adolph. These fears undoubtedly were passed on to her child.

At age eleven Adolph was nearly beaten to death by his father. Adolph's mother, according to those in the home, never stepped in. Adolph was uncertain who he was, and he had no faith his parents would save him; to the contrary his father nearly killed him. He was afraid of dying, and he was trapped. At any time his father could go into a rage and murder him, and his mother would not intervene. Hitler had no net, and he lived in an out of control environment.

Later, Hitler's sexual leanings shed light on his unconscious fears of loss of control. He gleaned sexual satisfaction from women squatting over him and urinating or defecating on his face. He became sexually excited when women kicked him. By asking for the abuse, by unconsciously requesting the abuse, Hitler gained control. In these moments, he was not terrorized by his mother's complacency, and he was in control of being treated like garbage.

Hitler's father died when he was 14, enabling Hitler to assume the patriarchal position. But he possessed no confidence. He was not programmed to believe anything or anyone would take care of him; his way of staving off the fear was to become monstrous and take control.

All emotions emanate from fear, and one of the most dangerous tentacles is rage. Hitler converted all his fears of death into a controlling obsession. After years of enduring his father's humiliation and torment, Hitler controlled fear by eliminating its sources. His rage reached across a continent and then the globe. He unconsciously attacked the source of his father's fears, and thus his father's rage, by attempting to eliminate the Jewish race. Hitler's father once locked Adolph in his room, when he learned he planned to run away; Hitler locked the Jews in concentration camps. Hitler ordered the Jewish population into death camps, terrorized and planned to eradicate them. His fervor was to control the world. He could not be controlled if he was God.

Under the Third Reich's euthanasia law, persons with mental illness were put to death, because Hitler believed they were "useless" in a "healthy" society. Hitler's maternal Aunt Johanna lived with Hitler throughout his childhood. She had a physical disability and schizophrenia. A person who appears to be mentally out of control adds fear to an already untenable environment. When drilling down, the reasons for Hitler's insanity is fairly transparent.

Mahatma Gandhi was born into the higher Bania Caste system in India. His family was distinguished, the previous three grandfathers having been prime ministers. His father was also in politics and was a prime minister. He described his father as having deep integrity and bravery but being short tempered. His father died when Gandhi was sixteen. Gandhi described his mother as a saint, she being deeply religious and knowledgeable about religion and politics.

Mahatma is considered one of the greatest spiritual leaders. He led with tacit non-violence. He gained strength through family privilege and his mother's spiritual devotion. Significantly, Gandhi had deep faith in his elders. They provided him sense of control and foundation. Gandhi once said, "I was blind to the fault of elders." In saying he was blind to the fault of his elders, he suggested he had unfettered faith in his base. He was confident he was protected. For Gandhi, truth was another faith, and black and white truth provided further unwavering control. When issues are black and white there is greater sense of control; vagueness suggests less control. Individuals who like a black and white world, a right or wrong world, likely feel less control.

Gandhi, like other great leaders, possessed a strong family foundation, a sense of privilege, a strong and supportive mother and the loss of his father at a relatively young age. Gandhi also endured personal challenges, including his own arranged marriage at 13 and the adjustments and hurdles that presented.

Foundational issues and fear levels in leaders is utterly important and potentially devastating for a society. It is critical we understand how our leaders are built, with regard to foundation, control and fear. When we elect a representative, we are voting to implant that individual's history into our own.

Hitler got into power by convincing the constituency there was something to fear, and the only way to mitigate the fear was through abusive control. Hitler was only dangerous if he was supported and elected to office - and the masses put him into power. When people are fooled and get behind bigoted, fear mongering individuals who use control and unmitigated aggression to reach an end, hell can be the price.

THE BONOBOS

In the center of the African continent, buried deep in the jungle, is the Democratic Republic of the Congo. To the north is the Congo River, the deepest river in the world, which snakes back and forth across the equator and releases more water into the ocean than any other. The River, formed about one to two million years ago, separates land to the north and south. The division of land also separates two tribes of primates of the Genus Pan, apes that are nearly 98% genetically similar to human beings. The Pan (genus) does not swim well, so the river stands between the two sub-species; they have no interaction.

The Chimpanzees are north of the river, and they are aggressive. Male dominated troops form war parties and systematically set out to attack neighboring tribes. When members of the neighboring tribes are located, the chimps attack, hold down and kill the male inhabitants of the other tribe. They beat the females, kill infant chimpanzees and eat them, and rape the females.

To the south of the river are the Bonobos, a peaceful, female dominated culture. The Bonobos are nearly identical genetically to the Chimpanzees, but the Bonobos resolve conflict through sex, not aggression. When a male hints at violence, the females descend on him and suppress the violence. The Bonobos have sex nearly constantly. Bonobos have group sex, gay sex, oral sex and face to face sex. They French kiss. They have sex as introductions to one another, sex when they find food and sex when they are anxious. They have sex in the trees, on the ground and in the water. They are one of a couple species that appear to have sex for entertainment and not just procreation. They share everything and fight over practically nothing. The Bonobos have evolved as lovers, not fighters.

CHAPTER TWENTY

ANIMAL KINGDOM

Man is rated the highest animal, at least among all animals who returned the questionnaire.

-Robert Brault

Much can be learned about human behavior from anthropology and the animal kingdom. The brain has many fundamental similarities to the brains of other species; the human brain is essentially built upon the brains of lower species. Our brains have evolved and advanced in aptitudes and cognition; conversely, we may have lost functioning in our other areas, such as in the olfactory and auditory senses.

When we look to the most basic forms of life, like a one celled amoeba, we begin to understand the base actions of all beings. An amoeba is drawn to stimuli that promote life, such as food sources and light and will withdraw from adverse stimuli, such as touch or threat from another organism. The basic functions of the amoeba are propagation of life and avoidance of death. Fear and control are the most elemental principles for survival.

While the lion sits atop the Kenyan wildlife food chain, it is still focused on survival. Lions are programmed to stay alive and procreate. Fear drives the lion, just as fear drives all species. Sustained lack of water for a lion will result in death, just as the crocodile waiting in the shallow waters of a pond also must eat to stay alive. Dehydration is guaranteed death, so level of thirst will determine whether the lion ventures to the watering hole full of crocs.

Water buffalo have injured and killed lions, yet when fear of starvation is greater than fear of potential harm from the water buffalo, lions will take calculated risks and go after a young water buffalo. The degree of fear determines the degree of control necessary.

A deer, recognizing it has been identified as potential prey, experiences raw fear. We know this fear; layered beneath years of evolutionary advancement, it is part of who we are. While the necessity of that evolutionary fear is not as consistently critical as it once was, we still allow fear to engage daily. Usually, it is misplaced into road rage, work "emergencies" and responses to social pressures. If the hunted deer doesn't run and zigzag and jump higher and faster than its foe, it will perish. Our work emergency typically will not truly result in death, but the trigger response remains, and unless we override with intellect, it still takes us.

While there clearly are differences, domesticated dogs and cats are essentially the same as those in the wild. It is easy to observe fear responses in animals in the home. Dogs not fearful are typically well managed. Some animals, such as pit bulls, are higher strung and, therefore, respond more quickly to threat. A dog in fear will snap into rage or aggression more quickly. It may not seem so to the casual observer, but fear is the impetus that drives an animal to attempt to control. The fear will look like aggression, but is really self-preservation tripped by fear.

A cat may first run, but if cornered or pursued it will fight. Fear converts to attempts to control. The intensity of fear correlates with the perceived immediacy of death. A cat may hiss when a dog approaches, when the cat does not feel imminent danger. It recognizes the vulnerability and possibility of danger, so it warns the dog. A prickle of fear may cause the hiss, but the cat may not attack. It has greater opportunity to escape death if it retreats and warns the dog off. If the dog approaches the cat will hiss and claw, and while this will look like aggression, it is really fear.

A lion, sitting high on a craggy bluff just after a meal, appears majestic and smug. The lion is not driven, at that point, to hunt for food. It is sated. Fear of dehydration and starvation are low. There is no threat from its perspective and, thus, no need to control. Relative absence of fear in a lion may look like pride, but those are humanizing projections of emotions. There is fear, and then there are varying degrees of absence of fear.

The otter's appearance of love and play is really absence of fear. Play is practice for fighting, escaping and survival. Otters and squirrels chase each other because they are farther down the food chain and need to learn escape. So, play is really conversion of fear into preparing for survival.

Trust is near absence of fear. When fear is low, and there is repeated and reinforced absence of fear around another, sense of trust is the result. When fear is high, sense of trust is low. Trust emerges when fear is minimized over time, which is why trust is so important in love. Reduction of trust increases fear, and fear blocks sexual feelings and abilities. When fear is abated, sexual union is more likely.

The basis for trust is developed early in all animals. The bonding that occurs between a mother and infant is important in predicting trust in adulthood. Regina Sullivan showed, in studies with rats, the amygdala functions or fear levels of the brain are substantially reduced when the mother is present. Fear activity in the amygdala automatically increases when the animal leaves the nest alone to investigate. This occurs whether or not there is an active threat. Bonding occurs with lower fear activity in the amygdale, when the mother is with its offspring. The result of bonding is creation of a loving relationship. And with such relationship, trust builds. Therefore, in healthy mother-infant relationships, the suppression of fear allows development of trust for others. Conversely, when abuse occurs, trust does not develop, and development of trust with others is damaged.

The infant who does not perceive he will be cared for has higher anxiety and fear response; he recognizes he must control the environment himself if he is to survive. He cannot rely on another. Nobody else is going to protect him. When trust does not develop, neither does confidence. Higher level mammals develop trust the same way human beings do. When bonding fails and trust is not established, fear never shuts off; the need to control intensifies.

Animals seem to have personalities, some more laid back than others. The development of trust and the lesser need to over-control is at the base of these appearances. We are animals, no different in many ways than other species, and our mechanisms for trust and confidence are mainly the same.

SANDLOT

The metallic, gold Rolls Royce was Jake's favorite. The chassis was soft on the suspension. The doors and the trunk opened and closed. "Move the dirt this way. Right here."

Chad dropped the shovel on the earthmover. He pushed. "Vroooooom. Vrooom." He kept his forefinger down, so the soil moved. "Kerrrrrr."

"No, this way," Jake corrected him. "Clear it to my mansion. "Yes. Like that."

Chad's eyes grew larger, and his concentration tightened, as he pushed the dirt ahead, observing the level indentation the shovel made in the earth. He peeked at Jake for approval, and proceeded up the incline to a small mesa.

"Not there. The built-in pool is going there."

"Oh," Chad responded, having no idea about a pool. "It's going to be cool."

Jake lined up his Matchbox cars. Jaguar. Lotus. Cadillac. Masserati. Rolls Royce.

"Hey." The voice was small behind them.

"Hey, Summer," Chad said, squinting into the sun.

"Whatcha doing?" Summer's short, dark hair hung into her face.

"Playing cars. We are going to have a mansion."

"Can I play?"

Jake didn't look up. "This is a boy's game. You wouldn't get it. See ya."

Summer stood there for a moment, not wanting to acquiesce to Jake. Then she spun, kicking sand over the road. "It's a stupid game anyway. I don't want to play." And she sulked off.

CHAPTER TWENTY ONE

WORKPLACE

A man without fear cannot be a slave.

-Edith Hamilton

For those of us with traditional careers or jobs, much of our lives are spent at work. Control is rampant, and because most of it is subconscious, much of what goes on isn't overtly known. It is, however, a critical dynamic in the workplace.

Control occurs from the board room to the water cooler. In meetings, control may manifest in an employee hogging all the time, talking over people. In covert ways, employees may be vying for position, calculating strategies for advancement, sometimes at the expense of others. Consider the following:

The CEO calls a meeting to order. He passes out an itinerary, identifying the objectives of the meeting. "Good morning," he begins. "This should be a quick meeting; there isn't a lot on the agenda, and Andy and I have another meeting at 10:30. Attached to the itinerary is a spreadsheet showing our quarterly earnings, which addresses the first agenda item. As you can see, we're taking a bath on domestic sales, but European sales are up 12%." The CEO goes into some detail regarding this then announces a meeting has been scheduled to drill down on the domestic numbers. "Jack, will you talk a bit about what is happening on the European front?" Jack starts by saying, "All I know is a number of my European co-workers are drinking a lot of wine and are never available until after 9 a.m." He chuckles, and the others at the table laugh, as well. (Humor is high level management of anxiety and temporarily dissipates fear. The greater the response from others, the more intense was the fear level.) "We have a slightly different product in the European market," he resumes. Jen, who has been with the company 2 years shy of Jack, speaks up, cutting him off. "This is more than just a product issue," she offers. "I've been researching some demographic information, and there's evidence at least part of the increased sales is due to an economic cycle." Jack waits politely for a pause, and then picks up where he left off, only to be interrupted again.

There are several examples of control in the synopsis, above. The CEO's opening of the meeting and taking control is appropriate. He is in charge of the meeting, and the expectation is that he will take control. Further, the itinerary outlines the meeting and builds parameters. The building of parameters is positive, because it established guidelines, and everyone wants predictability (control) and rules to mitigate spinning out of control. (Driving down a freeway without dividing lines or retaining walls is frightening; we want to know controls, through predictability, are in place.) The CEO's announcement another meeting was scheduled, which might interfere with the current meeting, also provides guidelines. When Jack speaks, he uses humor to reduce tension. He is in control but mitigates the level of control by use of humor. Then Jen interrupts – always a control move. She is attempting to focus attention on herself, while slightly undermining Jack. This is passive-aggressive control, and generally is not healthy. Jen's need to be in control suggests she has relatively high fear levels and is overcompensating for her own feelings of being out of control. A deeper look at Jen's upbringing and family history likely would provide answers as to why her response is so aggressive.

Control in the workplace can be overt and clearly aggressive or tacit and relatively passive. Talking over co-workers is exertion of control, but there are other more subtle behaviors. Walking ahead of a co-worker while talking with the person, so there is a need to skip forward in order to keep up, is controlling. Behaviors that are passive-aggressive, such as not asserting an issue, but rather sabotaging a co-worker's work, is controlling.

Sexual harassment in the workplace is defined as unwelcomed sexual advancement or comment that creates a hostile work environment. It is not asking for a date or offering an offhand, teasing comment; it is the creation of an environment that is uncomfortable. Sexual harassment is always a means of control. The perpetrator typically is intending, consciously or not, to manipulate the victim. A man may aim to back a woman off, intimidate her or make her feel inferior and out of control. "I really like the way that skirt makes your assets work," is really not a compliment. It says, you are a sexual object, and you are here for my enjoyment. I am in control, and you are not. You are less than I am, so I am superior to you. As such, I feel in control of you, mitigating my own fear of not having control.

Control can be taking hostage your time. A person who clearly overstays a welcome or continues to talk when several non-verbal or verbal cues are provided is controlling. This may not be malicious, but it is an exercise of control. The only thing any of us truly has is time, and abducting one's time is clearly controlling. Taken further, fear is about time on Earth being halted, so taking others' time can feel quite empowering.

Individuals working in reporting positions to yours in the company may make slightly disparaging comments, which are meant to control by bringing you down a level. The reason for the negative comments is based in fear of not having control. A confident individual, who perceives himself to be in control, will not make a comment denigrating another's position. Often negative comments will be delivered in the guise of humor, and while that does mitigate the blast, the intent is the same.

"I'm a little frightened you can't remember a meeting when you are in charge of the region. That's scary," the middle manager laughs. The statement is delivered under the guise of play, but the message is real. Otherwise, it wouldn't have been said. The intent is to bring you down a notch, so you are not as in control. If you are not confident, you may retort in a defensive manner. You might just let it go. Most important is to recognize it for what it is - an attempt to over-control, due to feeling a lack of control.

Leaders of organizations are in a different place, and leaders need to perform their duties with projections of control, if expected to be taken seriously. A leader in control will project calm. Eruptive leaders do not project calm or control. Strong leaders are predictable - though not to a fault - but a leader's course should be identifiable if he or she is going to be considered strong. Unpredictable behavior conjures fear and implies lack of control. Predictability in leadership is important, as is not waffling on a decision. Constituents want to see stability. If you are particularly good at inductive reasoning, or putting together the outcome based on the parts as they are coming together, and you know what's going to happen next, you will appear to be calm. Leaders who speak with even tone and maintain strong eye contact project confidence. Everybody loves confidence and wants to be around others who are confident, because it makes them feel there is control.

Leaders who lack confidence will over-control with threats. A leader who fires employees for frivolous reasons or makes threats of firing is really overcompensating for fear of losing control. A CEO who makes threats of any kind is generally overcompensating. Most employees know, through reason or company policy, what is expected of them. That doesn't mean expectations of behavior and performance should not be addressed; they should. But most are aware what will get them fired. To threaten recourse as a leader is to reveal weakness and fear of lack of control.

Leaders need to project control even when there is no clear answer. People want to feel safe, believe the leader understands and is on top of the situation. Indecision from a leader projects he or she is not in control. Sometimes making a clear decision based on sound reason and judgment is more important than getting everything perfectly right at every turn. Apologies should come only when there is clear reason, not when someone is unhappy with your decision. An apology can suggest a leader is questioning his own decision. If you work for a Board, be aware the more fearful the Board becomes, the more controlling the Board will be (micromanaging). A Board comfortable with a leader will provide room. A Board fearful will over-control - keeping in mind their fear may be coming from somewhere other than your leadership style.

Understanding at a conscious level what is going on is key. You cannot reason or plan or strategize if you are in the dark about what is happening. If you do not understand the dynamics operating in your office or in your relationships you cannot make necessary changes. It is discovery and knowledge that provide for possible redirection.

THE RIVER

There are places along the Au Sable River in northern Michigan, where you can stand and the cool water will come to just below your knees, tickling and undulating at five to six miles per hour. Even if you remain completely still, each passing minute puts you in a different world. Our world moves past us, changes, whether or not we participate.

Rivers move constantly, a physical and metaphoric slice of our world. Nothing is stagnant. Molecules change. The life forms within change. Borders of rivers erode and tumble in, tree roots are exposed and trees topple. Constant change.

Rocks formed millions of years ago, situated on the riverbed, partially buried, are polished by the moving water. The rocks erode. Change shape. The river courses over them, everything evolving.

Rivers shift. Satellite images of the Nile show the river has moved west nearly 30 miles in the past 5,000 years. Over time, rivers run more slowly. Slopes of riverbeds decrease; the depth of a river cannot be deeper than the surface of the body of water into which it flows.

Change comes, exposing those knee deep legs to a different environment, as each minute passes and each drop of water courses toward its objective.

CHAPTER TWENTY TWO

CHANGE

We wish to understand change in large part because we want to control it or – at the very least – to be prepared for its impact when it lies beyond our control.

-Michael Mahoney

Change is frightening. Change is constant and necessary, but change always unnerves people. Change, by definition, is about falling out of control, deviating from a known course.

The most stressful events for people include significant changes. Death of a loved one, divorce, moving, onset of illness and job loss are recognized as the top stressful life events. All signify substantial impending change, and all suggest loss of control. The death of a loved one not only indicates change is coming but erodes the illusion of immortality. Stress is a persistent, modulated fear. The fear is arising from the loss of control introduced by change.

In the book "Who Moved My Cheese," Spencer Johnson uses metaphor to discuss change. He suggests embracing change, because change is going to occur whether or not it is embraced. While he doesn't explicitly indicate, Johnson is implying change cannot be controlled. Change is, in fact, the loss of control. Johnson suggests individuals should maintain faith things will ultimately go well, rather than dwelling on the paralyzing realization things are changing. At a deeper level, Johnson is touching on the recognition of being out of control, becoming fearful and then over-controlling. Johnson's remedy is to not over-control but to have faith things will improve. This supposes, however, that having faith is just an activity.

Johnson's advice is good, if not over-simplified. Change causes fear but change is not the foundational fear. Fear of loss of control is beneath the fear of change. The perceived need to control is built on fear. And that fear is about death. Change makes us feel out of control, because we are unable to predict outcomes, and we don't know where the path before us is leading. Only the change is conscious. The rest is happening at an unconscious level.

Taking an alternate path can be emotionally tricky. Some leaders create change for the sake of change. If you are the leader, and you are orchestrating change, you are in control. Or so the illusion goes. A leader who is always pushing change without strong fundamental reasons, likely has reasons, and those reasons are probably rooted in the unconscious need to stay in control.

The child of an alcoholic grows up not being able to predict his environment. He tries. He becomes hyper-vigilant about the time his father arrives home, the weight of the slamming front door, the cadence of the steps – either he has been drinking or he hasn't. But that still might not be enough to predict, and prediction with individuals who tend toward violence is not just an academic exercise. It could mean life or death.

Thomas Hardy was 12 years old when he lived on Bacon Street on the southeast end of Chicago. He was the middle child, Chad being two years older and Sara 3 years younger. His father worked for the railroad, and his hours were erratic. His mother stayed home with the children and seemed to constantly be cleaning or cooking or doing something that required activity. She never sat. When he drank, and Mr. Hardy drank often, he was mean. He took it mostly out on his wife, but the kids were not spared his wrath.

Thomas knew the evening of December 22, 1974 was not going to be a good night. It was the last shift before the holiday break, which meant his father would be out drinking.

His mother's tone earlier on the telephone suggested fear, and when his father's prized Corvette rumbled up, and the front door opened at 2:38 a.m., Thomas knew. The door came back into the wall, so his father was either so sloppy drunk he couldn't maintain the door or he didn't care whom he woke. His steps were uneven on the wood floor, and when he fell into the stair rail, the goddammit that rolled off his tongue seemed accusatory. Thomas was scared. He was mostly afraid for his mother, but he feared for the entire household. It was a desperate move, but he had to do something.

Thomas Hardy was considered intelligent by his teachers, but over the past year he had had his share of run-ins with staff. Mostly administration. Specifically male administrators. Following what Thomas thought was an unfair grade on an assignment, the teacher's grade book was found in the waste can with several pages torn out. A student said she saw Thomas with the book. Thomas was suspended, and later the assistant principal's car was discovered with two flat tires. Nobody ever pinned that to Thomas, but few questioned who had done it.

When Thomas' father reached the top step he tripped on something. "I'm so fucking tired of this shit," he exploded. Then the door to his parents' room slammed open against the wall. Thomas heard his mother call out his father's name, in a meek voice.

Thomas had run this through his mind many times, but he didn't actually remember carrying out the events when later questioned. He didn't deny it. He knew he'd done it. He just had no recollection. He knew he had done it because the can of gasoline and knotted strip of bedding sheets he had hidden in the back of the coat closet were gone.

Thomas was certain he had soaked the scraps of tied sheets in gasoline before piping the cotton rope into the gas tank of the black Corvette. He had dumped the remainder of the contents of the can inside and all over the exterior of the new sports car. He did remember all the EMS vehicles, the red and blue lights flashing, the crowd gathering, the fire-hose torrent beating down the flames. He remembered his dad's rage, his mother's bleeding lip. And he recalled telling police, who were familiar with the residence, that his father had set the fire after trying to kill his mother.

Thomas' father was arrested. He never returned home. And, at a conscious level, Thomas was aware he had everything to do with his father leaving the house. He was not aware, however, that creation of chaos would continue into his adult life and be his mode of operation whenever he felt out of control.

In 2004, Thomas Hardy took the position of CEO for a bakery which sold to grocery stores chains across the United States. When revenues began falling dramatically, Hardy began to reorganize. He became myopic, evaluating his managers' clock hours and firing those managers not at the 85th percentile in hours worked. He shut down the third shift and laid off a third of his hourly workers. The bakery fell behind and was unable to make orders. Accounts were lost. Most knew his approach made no sense, but nobody dared step in. In 2007 the company declared bankruptcy.

Hardy's need to create chaos, to promote loss of control, was established as a young teenager. He learned to mitigate loss of control by creating chaos. Change is inevitable, but change created by an out-of-control leader is dangerous.

Our need for predictability and control leads to involvement and fascination with astrology, horoscopes, tarot cards and spirituality. We want to be able to predict, because it makes us feel in control. If you place no credibility in your daily horoscope, you may still take a peek, because there is strong desire to be able to predict the future. Horoscopes dot nearly every newspaper in America. Tarot readers are often not taken seriously, but we all know of people, perhaps including ourselves, who have visited soothsayers.

Inability to predict – to be able to anticipate the course - suggests change and loss of control. Relatively healthy individuals will control where they can. Unhealthy people will try to over control. Change may, indeed, be inevitable, but change is not always good. Change must be approached carefully and must be implemented for the right reasons. Change for the sake of change will inevitably cull anxiety and fear. When change in an organization is imperative, talking with employees about their anxiety will help mitigate the fear. Talk about those pieces that still are predictable. Reduce the fear through whichever avenues are available. The alternative, being unaware and ignorant of the effects of change, will definitely result in layers of over-control, from the top or within the organization.

WAR AND BENEFITS

world war II: **60 MILLION TO 85 MILLION KILLED WORLDWIDE** genocide: **6 MILLION JEWS** american civil war: **620,000 DEAD** rwanda genocide: **SYSTEMATIC, BRUTAL, MASS GENICIDE AND RAPE** rwanda deaths: **800,000** rwanda forearm amputations: **350,000 TO 1 MILLION** wwi deaths: **20 MILLION LIVES** mongol conquests: **40 MILLION TO 70 MILLION KILLED** three kingdoms war: **36 MILLION TO 40 MILLION DEAD** second sino-japanes war: **25 MILLION DEAD** taiping rebellion: **20 MILLION TO 100 MILLION DEAD HUMAN BEINGS** bosnian war rapes: **20,000** germans raped during wwii: **190,000** lushan rebellion: **13 TO 36 MILLION KILLED** conquest of the Americas: **8 MILLION TO 138 MILLION KILLED** dungan revolt: **8 MILLION TO 21 MILLION KILLED** conquests of tamerlane: **8 MILLION TO 20 MILLION KILLED** chinese civil war: **8 MILLION DEAD** russian civil war: **5 MILLION TO 9**

MILLION SLAUGHTERED napoleonic wars: **3.5 MILLION TO 6 MILLION KILLED** thirty years' war: **3 MILLION TO 11.5 MILLION LIVES** second congo war: **2.5 TO 5.4 MILLION KILLED** goguryeo sui war: **2 MILLION KILLED** shakas conquest: **2 MILLION LIVES** korean war: **1.2 MILLION LIVES** siege of jerusalem: **1.1 MILLION DEAD** mexican revolution: **1 TO 2 MILLION SLAUGHTERED FATHERS AND BROTHERS** iran-iraq first war: **1 MILLION KILLED** japanese invasion of korea: **1 MILLION DEAD** biafra war: **1 MILLION KILLED** soviet war in afghanistan: **1 MILLION TO 1.6 MILLION SLAUGHTERED** conquests of mehmed ii: **873,000 LIVES** seven years war: **868,000 TO 1.4 MILLION DEAD SOLDIERS** vietnam war: **800,000 TO 3.8 MILLION LOST THEIR LIVES**

CHAPTER TWENTY THREE

WAR AND POLITICS

Never think that war, no matter how necessary, nor how justified, is not a crime.

-Ernest Hemingway

Control does not just affect workplace relationships and board room conversations. It is not only about domestic violence and serial murder. It molds more than the movies we watch and sports we cheer. The drive to control shapes world politics, chokes out liberty and fans the flames of conflict that roar into world war.

Hitler was not the only man who, through childhood desperation to control, attempted to take over the world.

There have been plenty of malicious leaders, from Stalin to Mussolini, Napoleon to Kim Jong-il. History is rife with examples of policies and wars emanating from the drive to control. While control is not necessarily bad, it can lead to global catastrophe. Sometimes control is believed necessary to sustain life, and if control is truly an attempt to maintain existence or status quo, and not over-control to compensate for excessive fears, the attempts are just. But control shapes every decision. And unless you are aware of its existence, you cannot understand its potential for negative consequence.

Control is at the core of every war known to man. World War I was no different. The Hapsburg Empire, a conglomeration of states centered in Austria, wanted to be rid of its occupants, to regain control of its land. During the American Civil War, the south wanted to maintain control of slaves, and the north was bent on taking the control away. The 100 years war was about control of the throne and of land.

Policies and laws are developed as means of control. Prohibition was about controlling the behavior of the masses, and current drug laws do the same. Pharmaceutical companies lobby hard (controlling the legislature) to pass laws allowing legal provision for drugs. Child labor laws protect children, so ill willed employers cannot control youth and increase profits on the backs of the vulnerable.

The Iran-Contra Affair, on its surface, was about the sale of arms to Iran in exchange for hostages. But the ordeal ran much deeper, and the operational controls were significant. Iran was holding American hostages in Lebanon. The Iranians and the Lebanese feared the power of America and the west, and therefore set out to compensate by kidnapping and holding American hostages. The United States was willing to provide Iran arms for assistance in freeing the hostages. The United States also hoped the money received from the deal could be used to fund, in another part of the world, the Nicaraguan Contras. The Contras, in Honduras, were waging a military assault on the guerrilla government in Nicaragua, and the United States was trying to control the outcome. The American legislature, however, in attempts to control the intelligence arm of the government, prohibited funding the Contras. The intelligence community, attempting to hem in the legislature, tried to glean money to circumvent law and effect the over-throw of the guerrilla government in Nicaragua. It was a labyrinth in an abyss of attempts to control.

Politics is always about control. And it is driven by fear. The latent fear of death looms, and politicians set laws that control and box people in. They control the moves of other nations through threats of war or sanctions or nuclear power. While terrorist activities are rogue and savage, prosperous nations use more tacit threat. Terrorists hit and run, because they currently have no overarching threat to administer.

War is the ultimate attempt at control, when all other means of control appear to be exhausted. War for a nation is akin to homicide for an individual. War is imposed when control seems, otherwise, elusive. The nation feeling threatened will launch itself against the opposition. War is the homicidal-suicidal gesture of a nation, sometimes through one powerful leader.

In his book, "What Causes War?" Greg Cashman discusses theories of conflict. The book provides a thoughtful and well researched dissertation on why human beings enter into war. Cashman explores the aggressive nature of animals and human beings and provides substantial examples of primate groups fighting other groups. He explores the psychological impact of leaders and infers leaders with psychiatric illness may put a nation at greater risk of war. Put another way, leaders who are emotionally out of control pose great risk to the rest of the world.

While most of us believe war is atrocious and vile, it is an accepted part of our society. Wars have been erupting since the beginning of human existence, and we often glorify war. Theater and film romanticize the struggle and bore down to individual relationships. It is the dramatic backdrop for defiance, integrity, spirit and bravery. But the base reality of war is that it is the most dehumanizing, grotesque display of social interaction known to man. In World War II alone, an estimated 52,000,000 lives were lost. That represents 16% of the current population of the United States, including every man, woman and child. This number does not, of course, include numbers of individuals seriously injured and psychologically traumatized. What causes us to murder, to wage war and ultimately annihilate others in our species?

I believe Cashman is correct in his surmising war is based in aggression and is significantly affected by leaders with psychiatric illness. But what leads to aggression, and what drives the man with psychological demons to wage war on others?

Control. War is about maintaining or obtaining control. That control can emerge through an individual, like Hitler, wherein the leader himself was so desperately out of control, or the fear can be about loss of land, of freedom or of national respect. But the fear is about losing control, and war is an all out attempt to regain control.

Ignorance of the effects of control, the dynamics of fear and the control response, is dangerous. While all war and conflict may not necessarily be averted, knowledge about how control works to shape and create conflict is imperative.

SURVIVAL

Aron Ralston is an outdoorsman. By day he was an engineer, but he loved the outdoors and the challenges of hiking and climbing rocks. It was a typical day in Utah, when Ralston set out to hike Blue John Canyon. He liked being alone, enjoyed the solitude of walking and breathing in the fresh air. So, that morning in April, 2003, he didn't let anyone know where he was going. He was climbing down inside a narrow opening in the rock, when a boulder he was holding onto dislodged and came down on top of his right hand. He could not budge the 800 pound rock. Nobody knew where he was. He was trapped.

For five days he sipped the small amount of water and nibbled the little food he had with him until it ran out. His attempts at extricating his hand were futile. He was reduced to drinking his urine for hydration. He considered amputating his hand but had no tools to cut through bone. Fearing he would not survive the night, he etched his name and birth date into the stone. He videotaped goodbyes to his family.

Upon waking the next morning, he had an epiphany and leveraged his arm against the stone, breaking his ulna and radius bones. He applied a tourniquet. Then, over the next hour, using the dull blade of the multi-use tool he had carved his initials into stone with, he amputated his forearm. Weak and having sustained significant blood loss, he rappelled down 65 feet of sheer rock face and began his 8 mile walk back to his truck. Along the way, he ran into a couple and their son, who contacted authorities who rescued him by helicopter.

Ralston survived and went on to write the book "Between a Rock and a Hard Place," which reached number three on the New York Times Bestseller List. Ralston currently works as a public, motivational speaker.

PART FOUR

THE SETTLING

CHAPTER TWENTY FOUR

RESOLVE

I cannot change what will happen. I can only change how I act in the face of it.

-Robert Fanney

Throughout this book, I have attempted to demonstrate that, as a human species, we keep hidden our abject fear of death and respond to such fear with attempts at control. In order to maintain the illusion of immortality, we bury the fear of death deep in our collective unconscious. If we were to continually think about our mortality, we would be paralyzed. For some, whose anxiety bleeds through, attempts at control manifest in obsessive-compulsive behaviors and other neuroses. In order to suppress fear, we live the illusion we are in control. Our society projects this illusion through film, amusement parks, books, sporting events and architecture. When fear of death or loss of control presses us, we assert greater control. The level of control we attempt to assert is equal to the level of control we believe we are losing. The illusion of control mitigates fear of death. At the most extreme point on the continuum of fear, when we believe all is about to be lost, we are most vulnerable – and our actions potentially result in homicide, suicide or war.

Being in control all the time is exhausting, and while we are driven to control, we often resent it. We want to relax, to breathe and enjoy life. We dream of winning the lotto, not because of the physicality of money but because of the control and power money brings and the reduction of fear it provides. The fantasy is that if you win big there is never need to worry again. There is no need to obsess about work or the mortgage or taking a vacation. Everything is taken care of. All the anxiety and worry slips away. That is the illusion, anyway.

The good news, the powerful message I want you to hear, is we don't have to be in control all the time. Often, we just want to be taken care of, and that option is largely available. When we step outside our myopic worlds and observe the larger world, the universe, our need for control diminishes. There already exists great control in the universe. And therein lies the key to dissipating a large part of the stress and the need to control.

Strong leaders tend not to over-control. Strong leaders possess confidence, an underlying sense there is foundation and existing control. Often, this sense is established early in life and is based on generations of aristocracy and wealth or spiritual or religious conviction. The confidence comes from strong foundation and belief there is control in the world, that there is a natural net.

Individuals with deep religious faith, regardless of faction, endure less stress and anxiety than control groups. The foundational support believers enjoy relieves them of need to be in control. In a study of brains of individuals with deep religious conviction, Michael Inzlicht demonstrated, through brain imaging, that people who believed in God had significantly reduced brain activity in the anterior cingulated cortex (ACC). The ACC is a cortical system responsible for monitoring need for control and for increasing anxiety levels. So, people who deeply believe – not those using religion as a tool for manipulating or controlling others – have greater sense of calm, because they believe they have a net. They are confident there is control, so the need to over-control is mitigated.

Religion is spirituality, but being spiritual does not necessarily mean being religious. Opening one's self up to a spiritual world does not prescribe the way; it only suggests there is something larger than the physical world. The inability to see something does not preclude its existence. A person without sight knows there is a visual world, even though she cannot see it. We do not see ultraviolet and infrared colors, but we know the range exists.

Letting go of control is healthful. The National Institutes of Health research suggests that meditation reduces blood pressure, symptoms of irritable bowel syndrome, anxiety, depression, insomnia and severity of some viruses. Meditation is the art of letting go, of relaxing the mind and delving into the unconscious. One of the positive aspects of meditation is looking within, without judging what is found. Meditation is antithetical to over-control.

Rarely is fear, the fear that drives our systems into survival mode, necessary. Office politics is unlikely to be mortally dangerous. The ride home, while annoying, won't usually kill you; your inattention on the road, however, may, as may manifesting over-controlling through road rage. Most of us are not facing life threatening situations on a daily basis, yet our bodies are responding as though we are.

When you feel emotion welling out of you, acknowledge fear is at the root. Try saying to yourself, in those situations, "No fear." Say it over and over in your head. Push the fear down. Use your cognitive system to find solutions, and as the fear buds, repeat to yourself, "No fear." Allow your brain, your imagination, to consider alternatives. Keep working until you find something, but don't acquiesce to the fear. Fear will short-circuit your thought process and disallow solution processing.

The Twenty-First Century is shoving us farther away from our spiritual selves. Cell phones, computers, tablets and I-Tunes crowd our brains. People text at dinner and during conversations with others. Photos, tweets and Facebook document our every move, thought and plan. We live in a world that is not conducive to peace, calm or to letting go.

Spiritual integrity cannot exist with so much visual, auditory and mental encroachment. As we become more crowded, more peppered with stimulation, our need to control increases. In a well known study by John Calhoun, rats in overcrowded, over-stimulated conditions resorted to aggression and cannibalism, and infant mortality rose to 96%. When the need to control rises, spiritual sense diminishes.

Getting in touch with the non-physical self is an easy way to reduce the need to control. But you have to pull away from the noise. A quiet walk. Sitting alone. Getting in touch with your breathing and body through Yoga. Listening. Looking inward without self-judgment or self-castigation. Hear yourself. Understand how you fit into the universe. Quiet the noise.

If you don't want to study yoga or meditation, simply give yourself ten to fifteen minutes each day. Pay yourself first. Stand, sit or kneel in a quiet place. Close your eyes and imagine the totality of the universe. Breathe in the universe. Exhale stress. No fear. Stretch your muscles. Straighten your spine. Feel your muscles expand. Open. Breathe. Let go. Consider the oxygen you inhale, provided to you, a part of you, because you are part of the universe. No fear. Feel the fear come up and gently suppress it. Each day, take this time for yourself. Stretch. Breathe. Clear your mind. Push the fear down.

When we allow ourselves to see and understand the enormity of the universe, the breadth of the world, we understand there is something greater than we. Only quiet and humble acceptance we are part of something greater, be it God or nature or the universe, will allow us to let go. There is a fundamental control already in place; there is a net, and the net enables you to find peace.

CAUSATION

He steps up to the tee. The shoes are new, so he settles the cleats in a little deeper. The ball is lined up with his left heel. He takes a breath, his chest rises, and he breaks his wrists and pulls his arms back. His hips come back then forward, the man aware his left hip crossed the imaginary line perpendicular to the tee before his club struck the ball. He compensates, ever so slightly, lifting up an eighth of an inch. The clubface pings, his body attitude pulled marginally to the right and up. The ball comes off the tee straight then fades right.

• • •

In an industrial city in Asia fossil fuels lift into the air, changing to aerosol particles. The particles eventually develop into storm clouds that build and billow, then slowly move out over the Pacific Ocean. The clouds pick up warm updrafts from the water, stretch fat and black, rolling across the expanse of sea - and days later onto the California coast, where they begin to empty, as they slide east. Up over the Rocky Mountain Range the clouds absorb cold humidity, breeding more weather. Onto the plains and into the Midwest, the storm clouds race.

• • •

A gust of wind jumps across the fairway, ahead of the front moving from the southwest. The wind whirls and sends the airborne golf ball down and to the right. The dimpled sphere loops low, catching the branch on a Maple Tree, a branch extended a full inch the last two days, due to its flowering, springtime bud. The ball deflects, careens off the thick trunk of a nearby oak and stabs down into an acorn buried by a frantic squirrel in fall. The ball jumps out of bounds.

The man stands at the tee, leaning left in an attempt to persuade the ball. "Shit," he says, deflating, deprecating his lack of talent. "Dammit!"

CHAPTER TWENTY FIVE

DETERMINISM

To talk of probability is to suggest that events might happen differently from the way they do, whereas events themselves will unfold according to an inevitable path.

-Johnny Rich

When a cheetah gives chase, a gazelle will run. It appears to be a battle of wit, cunning and control. But that is an illusion, a fantasy. The gazelle's outcome is fixed.

The philosophical argument regarding free will is old. David Hume proposed we do not truly have free will; all factors were decided at the beginning of time and every following event occurs as a result of the actions set into place at that time. R.E. Hobart and William James essentially concurred but believed there was an element of chance in outcomes. The agreement between them, however, is that there is little choice, and we have little control in our lives. It is not a comforting concept, but if you follow the trail it becomes clear.

Consider the gazelle. Each animal possesses millions of years of biological heredity. The gazelle is wired in a very specific way, so the day of its birth it was equipped with a neurological-muscle-aptitude package. Each molecule of the gazelle is dependent on every minute affect on that mammal, before and after birth. That is fixed. Behaviorally, the gazelle learned from its parents, which learned from their parents, and was taught to run from predators. It learned where to eat and find water. The gazelle did not determine where it would be born, and where it would be at the moment the chase began. Its neurological, sensory and behavioral evolution all come together at the point the cheetah begins the hunt, and the gazelle runs. That's it. The neurological response is built on the precise biological make-up of the gazelle at that moment in time. The gazelle will respond, based on what it has learned and how it is biologically programmed. It can only play out in one way.

The human species is part of the animal kingdom; we share more with, than we differ from, other animals on the planet. We are wired much like other mammals, and while we possess much greater capacities, in some respects, we are nonetheless close genetic cousins to other species on the planet. The DNA code of a chimpanzee is nearly identical to human beings.

As human beings, we are able to reflect on our past and predict, with some accuracy, the future. We know that if we throw a hard ball at a window, the window will break. We do, therefore, possess prognostic capabilities. We understand cause and effect. On the other hand, we get caught up, at times, in what-if thinking. How often have you thought, if I'd only done it this way I wouldn't be in the predicament I'm in? If I hadn't accepted that first cigarette from my friend, I wouldn't be a smoker today.

The choice seems clear; having the choice is an important part of the illusion of control. But the level of control is not as simple as we would like to believe. There are millions of years of evolution and programming in each individual, which culminates in the decision made at any given point in time. There are thousands of behavioral experiences that come into effect at the time a "decision" is made. Millions of years of genetic and biological predisposition drive our actions. As on a roller coaster ride, we don't have the ability to determine where the track will lead us, whether we will loop up or down, to the left or right; the destination is fixed. We are able to control our movement, to a certain extent, within the car. That is about the extent of our ability to make choices, to exercise control, over our lives. That is a frightening concept, but any indication we don't have control is frightening, by its very nature. This concept may also conflict with your religious convictions, but even in the Bible and other religious texts there are indications of this. Your path is known by God. Ancestors determine your fate. The Bible, in Isaiah 46:10 offers that God is, "...declaring the end from the beginning and from ancient times things not yet done." Similarly, in the Quran, 13:9, Allah, "...is the Knower of the future and unseen and the witnessed, the Grand, the Exalted."

Consider the following: Pick a goal you believe you should have attained or would like to have accomplished. Let's say the goal was to graduate from Harvard University with a PhD in Musical Composition. Consider the goal, as you check through the series of your pseudo-life events. Ask yourself, given the conditions, how likely were you to reach your goal given the conditions:

- You were born in Thailand

- You're mother worked as a prostitute in order to provide for you and your six siblings
- Your father has been in prison for as far back as you can remember
- The year is 1877
- You have never been afforded formal education
- Your home is made of thatch and the floor is dirt
- You spend much of your time wondering when and from where your next meal will come
- You have been taught that minor thievery is a way of survival; just don't get caught

- You watched your younger sister die from malnutrition

- Your family accepts its lot in life

Obviously, these are extreme circumstances, but the point is, you had no choice (as far as I'm aware) where you were born, to which parents, to what level or class and at what point in history. And this is the basis, the foundation, upon which all other issues rest. You did not choose your intellect or whether or not you were born with a physical, cognitive or emotional challenge.

Control is a drive; but control is mostly an illusion. We maintain the delusion, because we deny, as a rule, that we are mortal. The delusion helps us get through each day and not focus on the reality of impending death. This unconscious drive to control, to be in control, as a means of denying our mortality, is sublimated through billion dollar industries of film, sports and architecture. Evidence of the collective unconscious drive of the human race is everywhere. It permeates our existence, seeps into every behavior, revealing itself in symptoms of over-control.

We paint an illusion of control, because the reality of our mortality and relative lack of control is frightening. You may be feeling on edge as you read this. You've come this far, so please read on. There is a silver lining.

CONSTELLATIONS

BY LOUEVA SMITH

My favorite color is navy blue,

the color of a childhood book about stars.

My father read it to me on the couch,

took me outside and showed me

the Big Dipper, and the Little Dipper,

and how to find the North Star.

All of this was right in front of our house.

We looked up into the sky until it looked

back.

The book said we spin without realizing it.

It told where we are in the Milky Way

but my father and I don't know how we

got here.

BONES IN A BOX

Neither of us mentions it.

We do not know how to do the math

on astronomical odds as big as that.

CHAPTER TWENTY SIX

NATURE

I felt my lungs inflate with the onrush of scenery—air, mountains, trees, people. I thought, 'This is what it is to be happy.'

-Sylvia Plath

Over-control comes from fear of losing control – those who have a poor foundation of trust and sense of being cared for are at greatest risk. The fear, of course, is about death. Individuals, who have deep foundations, generations of wealth and support – or religious or spiritual conviction, tend to be more relaxed and less controlling. The foundation of comfort, of nurturing, of having a net that keeps us from falling into the abyss is key. Typically, we tend to overlook the natural foundation all around.

Proof exists everywhere that nature is the net. There is a rich foundation of support, and we are, for the most part, being taken care of. The evidence is provided daily, yet we walk by without a glance, a whiff or cognitive recognition. Nature is a constant, supportive, nurturing structure. Many believe God is the underpinning of nature, and while this book is not about religion, the reality is the same. We don't have to be in control at the level we often perceive, because we are taken care of.

The air we breathe is provided. It's free. There is no response needed, no bill to submit, no thank you required. It is just there. The oxygen produced is emitted from trees and plants, generated through a complex system of ecological balance.

Trees have been growing for billions of years. These factories of air that sustain life are gifts. We do nothing to earn this essential component of life. Our greatest minds create medical instruments, airplanes and skyscrapers, but the elements we take for granted, those components essential for life, are far beyond our abilities of production. The very foundations of life that support our biological existence, which support procreation of all species, that sustain us through the entire life cycle are just provided. And while tsunamis and earthquakes and wildfires may blemish these gift, those events are anomalies in a system that provides general support for our existence. You may assert all these conditions exist, yet there are the atrocities of disease and horror all over the globe. And while this is correct, much of it is man-made; civil war, murder, hoarding of resources and the need to control, rather than to share, are all created by human beings. This is not the design of nature.

Year in and year out, throughout the existence of time, without your input or control, the seasons rotate and life unfolds. Trees and plants grow and regenerate, ferns poke and stretch through the forest floor and fruit miraculously appears for the sustenance of animals. When spring emerges, you can almost feel the gleeful gratitude of all species. Birds sing and activity bustles. There is a collective excitement for life. Disney's animated scenes of spring life are probably closer to reality than they are fantasy. The cycles of nature provide the open hands that hold us.

The human species can be brilliant, but we cannot manufacture water. It is a gift. Fresh water, trickling or rushing through woods and down mountains and into meadows, has been part of the system of Earth for as long as we have been here. There are draughts, and there are those who do not enjoy an abundance of fresh, clean water, but the essence and the creation of water is not something we control.

Water is essential to all life; it is a commonality across all species. Most species can go far longer without food than water, and yet species will fight over food but rarely over a body of water. Water is a shared commodity.

The eco-system which provides foundation for life is inarguably remarkable. Look at a hundred year old tree, a nugget of nature that stands as monument of the provisions of life we generally take for granted. If you look closely at the craggy ridges, the perfect imperfections of the bark, the skin, within which a network of arteries feed the organism, you recognize you are marveling at a biological miracle. We would not exist without the oxygen released from trees, and trees would not exist without birds and bees working harmoniously to maintain the ecosystem – the ecosystem which has operated for billions of years. Nature is evidence there is control, and we benefit from that control.

Unconsciously, we recognize the power of nature. But that recognition, too, is buried deep from our conscious minds. Meditation, yoga and other forms of relaxation take us closer to knowledge of the nurturing power of the universe, but our current construct of life, with aggressive business, cell phones, electronic bombardment and expectations of a maniacal pace, steals us away.

Take a deep breath. Breathe in the aroma of the budding trees, grass, flowers and vegetation. Listen to birds chirping or crickets singing. They are all reminders of the power of nature and reality we do have foundation; we can let go. Listening to nature, visualizing nature, provides relaxation, because we become aware we are not in control. We do not need always to be in control. That is precisely why relaxation sound tracks are nearly always recordings of the ocean waves, pattering rain, birds singing and crickets chirping. We relax when we understand there is a foundation of control protecting us.

When we lie on the beach, we relax. Our bodies give into the meditative rhythms. The sun warming our skin. The distinct fishy-salty smell of the ocean. Waves, rolling in and pulling back, water folding onto the sand, crawling up the beach, receding back. Seagulls call from a distance. There is a peace. Unconsciously, we recognize the ocean has done this for billions of years. The seas cover over seventy percent of Earth, support hundreds of thousands of life forms and have been licking the beaches of Earth from the beginning. When sitting at the edge of the ocean, we cannot deny we are part of something much larger. The world does not revolve around us; we are an infinitesimally small part of a colossal system. There is control. The oceans remind us with every lazy, folding wave that laps the sand. We need not attempt to control everything.

Sitting on the beach can be a spiritual event. Consciousness expands, and the need to control diminishes.

You breathe more deeply, more evenly and unconsciously float into the protective arms of the universe.

When we believe we are the center of everything, when we believe our position in the company or a club is critical to its function, we think we have to take control. Everything depends upon our work. That perspective induces fear. If we fail to perform well, the company or the club fails. The fear of not having control sits on deeper fears, and this increases stress levels.

Perspective is critical. A church, synagogue or mosque can provide perspective, and that is partly the reason we feel de-stressed after attending a service. The message is there is a higher control; and you are not in control. You are taken care of and can let go. If religious activity is not your way, find a place away from the city. Pick a warm summer evening. If you aren't averse to camping, pitch a tent. If you hate camping, find a cabin in the woods. On a clear night, lie on your back on a blanket next to a fire and gaze at the stars. It is awe inspiring. Most people never see the full constellation of stars because of city lights. When you view them in their totality, you cannot deny you are part of something so much greater that the need to control abates. You recognize you are infinitesimally small, but, moreover, you don't need to be in control all the time. There is control. The universe has been and will exist without your control. Stars have exploded and imploded and died. Some of the stars you see are no longer there; the light reaching you from a star may be millions of years old, but that star may no longer be. Planets have formed, solar systems have spun into existence and you recognize, at some level, you are a part of a very huge whole. The universe has been operating without you for billions of years, providing the foundation for your existence.

Have you wondered why the gentle, steady fall of summer rain is so relaxing? Smell the aroma. The patter is even and hypnotic. It feeds flowers, lawns and vegetation. It has for billions of years. And we have done nothing to promote it. Water falls from the sky, providing a life line, replenishing rivers, lakes and oceans. It provides relaxation, because unconsciously we understand we are being taken care of, provided for, sustained.

Most of us love infants, but relaxation sound tracks don't play sounds of infants crying or cooing. The image of an infant translates to our needing to be in control, our being the center of the universe. Conversely, the steady patter of rain reminds us we are part of something larger, and we are not in control. There is a control, and we can relax.

Watching birds, while seemingly out of vogue, can be quieting. Spotting robins and blue jays are peaceful, and it is because they represent and prove the cycle of life. Birds are descendents of dinosaurs, thus they have been around longer than most species. They are manifest indication of the control of the world, the billion year cycle of life and the sustainability of the earth. While some things need to be attended to, the underlying viability of life has been supported since before human beings were on the planet.

Appreciate the sun, the stars, lakes and rivers, oceans, trees and vegetation. Take hikes through the woods or the mountains. Integrate with nature and breathe. You are part of something much larger. Life does not revolve around you. You are cared for; and you need not always try to control.

Practice finding your center. Be one with the universe. Go to that place where you know yourself, where confidence springs. It is that place that is you. If you don't know that place, if you can't find the center, you must begin forgiving yourself for your perceived shortcomings. Be kind to yourself. Whatever transgressions you believe you have committed, whatever unforgiving deeds you've done, they are done. And you need to move forward. We are where we are; there is no taking that back. Consider taking classes in meditation and yoga. Practice a martial art, wherein your body and mind synchronize and focus on matters more spiritual. Spend ten to twenty minutes with yourself each morning stretching and breathing. These techniques have been practiced in the East for centuries, and the benefits are now being recognized scientifically.

Let go. Breathe deep. Relax. No fear. Find moments you are not in control and practice them throughout the day. Walk. Open your hearts and ears to nature, to the harmony of the universe. Live. Smile. Be at peace. No fear.

EPILOGUE

I am sure that everyone who writes a book believes the information being imparted is important. I'm no different. I've carried this book in my head for many years. I've applied its principles to nearly every situation, and the principles hold. I have challenged individuals in my profession to refute my findings, through logic and pragmatic approach, but I've been met with little argument.

Fear is the base emotion, sitting atop the fear of death, and our collective response is to attempt control. From the lowest form of life to the level of our human species, fear (or some form of switch that releases survival chemicals) causes the reaction of control. The stronger the fear, the greater the reaction.

It is a fundamental principle that explains the foundational dynamics of relationships, aggression, violence, war and the entire human experience. All emotions are based in fear, and the constructs of our society are built on the drive to control. Sexual fantasy carries the unconscious control drive, vacillating between controlling all and complete loss of control. Our entertainment is a projection of our need to control and our fear of losing control, and it explains our willingness to spend and partake, as an investment, in movies and professional sports. Murder, sexual assault, war, architecture and art are all mired in fear and control. But this is only the tip of the iceberg.

This book was meant to be a quick read, an introduction to a philosophy and principle which hopefully will garner more interest, introspection and research. Bones in a Box is the human skeleton of the foundation from which all emotions are derived, all actions rooted, from which all human propensity stems. The purpose of this book is not about self-righteous opinion or assertion, but rather about illuminating truth and better understanding what motivates and drives our behaviors. Knowledge bolsters our collective ability to correct errant directions and foster healthier decisions.

We are a brilliant people, but often we engage in behavior that would be shocking and appalling for even a lower life form. We murder. We rape. We wage war, suffering and torture upon one another, yet that is not what defines our species – or it is at least what should not define our species. We wrestle with our lower, animal brains, our limbic system, and forego the power of our smarter, more planful brains. There are so many things we do not understand; but knowledge and exploration help us all evolve and become more aware of our deficits.

I have deep faith in our species, yet when fear rises, when opportunities dim and desperation escalates, we devolve. We slip further into our fear responses and move farther away from our higher thinking abilities.

I apply the principles of this book to every situation in which I see controlling or out of control behavior, and in doing so it all makes sense. When emotions rise, when behaviors and decisions are difficult to understand, ask what is driving the fear. The fear may be emanating from you, your boss or co-worker. The emotion may be welling in personal relationships. What is driving the fear, and how is control being applied in an attempt to quell the fear?

I ask you not close this text and give no further thought, as the concepts in this book fade over night. I humbly request, of any who have interest, to build on this information, to open the shades and shed light on this subject.

Notes

INTRODUCTION

Sigmund Freud's theory of the Oedipus Complex is a controversial posit which proclaims boys have unconscious desire to kill their fathers and have sex with their mothers: *The Dissolution of the Oedipus Complex* (Standard Edition, 1924). Freud named the theory after Sophocles' *Oedipus Rex*, who kills his father and marries his mother.

Phillip R. Shaver and Cindy Harzan employed Positron Emission Tomography Scans (PET Scans) revealing the parts of the brain that light up when an infant son and mother are bonding is the same area of the brain activated when bonding occurs between sexual partners: "A Biased Overview of the Study of Love" in the *Journal of Social and Personal Relationships vol. 5, no. 4 (*November 1988): *473-501.* Oxytocin is the hormone involved in both bonding acquisitions.

Deborah Lipstadt provides a factual appraisal of the means and methods for the Holocaust denial in *Denying the Holocaust: The*

Growing Assault on Truth and Memory (New York: Plume/Penguin, 1994).

ONE: FEAR

Walter Bradford Cannon, MD, first described the fight or flight response in his book *The Wisdom of the Body* (New York: W.W. Norton & Company, Inc., 1932). Cannon was an award winning physiologist and Harvard professor.

Julio Rocha do Amaral, MD, and Jorge Marins de Oliverira, MD, PhD, describe the layers of the brain, establishing it as an archeological dig. Within the paleopallium (or old mammalian brain), being akin to the brain of inferior mammals, is the limbic system, responsible for emotions: "Limbic System: The Center of Emotions," published in *Mind and Behavior, Electronic Magazine on Neuroscience*, no. 5 (1998).

Brain studies reveal oxytocin reduces fear, thus applications for individuals with PTSD and autism, as well as others with generalized anxiety, are underway. Galen Messig, Luke Ayers, Jay Schulkin and Jeffrey Rosig describe startle responses being denigrated by oxytocin: "Oxytocin Reduces Background Anxiety in a Fear-Potentiated Startle Paradigm," *Neuropsychopharmacology*, 35 (13), 2000, 2607-2616. M. Henricks, B. von Dawans and G. Domes provide further evidence in:

"Oxytocin, vosopressin, and human social behavior," *Front Neuroendocrinol,* 30 (4), 2009, 548-557.

On December 16, 1998, Bill Clinton, after having been accused of an illicit relationship with Monica Lewinsky, was further accused of ordering the bombing of Iraq as a means of distracting constituents from the issue: *Clinton Orders Air Attack on Iraq.* See https://www.history.com/this-day-in-history.com.

Following the attacks of September 11, 2001, the economy crashed, as a result of many factors, including a two-front war with Iraq and Afghanistan. In addition to lives lost and injuries incurred (physical and psychological), the Dow dropped more than 600 points in one day, spending on security increased overwhelmingly and the total cost of the terrorist response came in at about $1.8 trillion: *How the 9/11 Attacks Still Affect the Economy Today.* See

http://useconomy.about.com.

THE RAVEN – BY EDGAR ALLAN POE

The excerpt of the Raven, Edgar Allan Poe's most famous poem, was originally published in the New York Evening Mirror on January 29, 1845: *Nevermore: The Edgar Allan Poe*

Collection of Susan Jaffe Tane. See http://rmc.library.cornell.edu/poe/exhibition/the raven/.

TWO: FEAR IS DEATH IS FEAR

Conversion Disorder, a Functional Neurological Symptom Disorder, is listed under the Somatic Symptom and Related Disorder section of the DSM-5. These disorders feature significant somatic symptoms and characteristics: *Diagnostic and Statistical Manual of Mental Disorders – Fifth Edition* (Arlington, American Psychiatric Association, 2013).

THREE: CONTROL

Emanuella Grinberg of CNN reported on Nik Wallenda, a seventh generation daredevil. On November 2, 2014 he performed a highwire act blindfolded, 600 feet above ground: *Nik Wallenda Completes Blindfolded Tightrope Walk in Downtown Chicago* (www.cnn.com/2014/11/02/travel/nik-wallenda-chicago).

Eric Jackson writes about narcissistic CEOs and the damage they do to companies in a January 2012 article: *Why Narcissistic CEOs Kill Their Companies* (www.forbes.com/sites/ericjackson/).

In the Leadership Quarterly, 2013, Charles O'Reilly, Bernadette Doerr, etal. show no correlation between highly compensated CEOs and business performance: (www.haas.berkeley.edu).

Tucker Vale is a variation of an individual situation about which I am personally aware. The individual and company names were changed to protect his identity.

New York Post writer Leonard Greene describes, in a May 13, 2015 article, the bizarre and disturbing executions ordered by North Korea leader Kim Jong-un: *Kim Jong Un Sends Brutal Message with Grisly Executions* (nypost.com/2015/05/13). Consistent with narcissistic personalities, Kim Jong-un demands admiration and adulation, without warrant.

FOUR: SUBLIMATION

Jerrold Maxmen, M.D. defines sublimation as a defense mechanism, whereby repressed need is satisfied through socially acceptable means: *Essential Psychopathology* (New York, W.W. Norton & Company, 1986).

Keith Schneider reports on the complicated life of Dr. Jack Kevorkian in a June 3, 2011 New York Times article: *Dr. Jack*

Kevorkian Dies at 83; A Doctor Who Helped End Lives. See http://www.nytimes.com/2011/06/04kevorkian.html.

Ben Carson, M.D. writes about his childhood and ascension to Director of Pediatric Neurosurgery at Johns Hopkins Hospital in his autobiography *Gifted Hands: The Ben Carson Story* (Grand Rapids: Zondervan, 1996).

FIVE: SPORTS

Plunkett Research shows the United States sports industry is worth nearly $500 billion and the global industry is valued at $1.5 trillion: (www.plunkettresearch.com/statistics/sports-industry/), numbers exceeding the GDP of Norway and the United States, respectively:
(www.tradingeconomics.com/country-list/gdp).

The President of the United States is provided a salary of $400,000 annually, up from $200,000 in the Year 2000: (www.presidentsusa.net/presidentsalaryhistory.html).

SIX: SEX

Sigmund Freud first proposed the theory of the id, ego and superego in1920 in *Beyond the Pleasure Principle*, but Freud expanded and tightened his theory in *The Ego and the Id* (London, Hogarth Press; Institute of Psycho-Analysis, 1927).

Martin Buber's deeply philosophical book *I and Thou* explores the human experience and interface with the world and others: (Leipzig: Insel Verlag, 1923).

Nancy Friday's *My Secret Garden* was an iconic and groundbreaking, bestselling compilation of women's sexual fantasies. The book drew controversy but was mostly received as a liberating release for women, normalizing their sexual fantasies (Pittsburgh: Pocket Books, 1973; RosettaBooks, LLC; 2013).

William Masters and Virginia Johnson revolutionized research on sexuality. Together, they observed and recorded sexual responses and were the first to identify the different phases of sexual orgasm, which is noted in their book *Human Sexual Response* (New York: Ishi Press International, 1966).

SEVEN: MOVIES AND OTHER ENTERTAINMENT

Ian Fleming wrote Casino Royale (Las Vegas: Thomas & Mercer, 1953) in two months and created an entertainment industry. J.K. Rowling wrote seven novels about Harry Potter and his wizardry, the debut novel being Harry Potter and the

Philosopher's Stone (London: Bloomsbury, 1997). Rowling, once a single mother on state assistance saw her novels and movies earn billions of dollars. The Raimis' Spiderman Trilogy, Hitchcock films, James Bond and Harry Potter movie series brought in billions of dollars at the box office (www.the-numbers.com/movies/franchise/).

Laura Hillenbrand's biography *Unbroken* (New York: Random House, 2010) depicts survival and will to survive. Peter Benchley's *Jaws* (New York: Doubleday; Random House, 1974), metaphorically drawing on fear hidden beneath the surface, stayed on the New York Times bestseller list for 44 weeks.

EIGHT: ARCHITECTURE

CNN writer Eoghen MacGuire, in her article *The Chinese firm that can build a skyscraper in a matter of weeks*, described the race to build China's Sky City, the tallest building in the world (www.cnn/2015/06/26/asia/china-skyscraper-prefabricated). They used 19 work days to erect the prefabricated structure.

James White identified the Khufuis Pyramid in his article World's Tallest Buildings in the BSHS Travel Guide, A Travel Guide to Scientific Sites, Nov 7, 2013 (http://www.bshs.org.uk/travel-guide/worlds-tallest-buildings).

NINE: VIOLENCE

Erik Strom was a visage created by the author, based on several stories that illustrated violent relationships. Strom typifies the love connection gone wrong. The vignette is the outline, the parameter, within which so many stories emanate.

Captain Chesley Sullenberg was a US Airways pilot with extensive experience, both as an airline pilot and as an Airforce fighter pilot and trainer. His experiences provided him direction and kept him calm in the face of potential calamity. Robert Kolker, in his article "My Aircraft:" Why Sulley May Be the Last of His Kind (New York News & Politics, Feb 09) writes about the calm demeanor and predictable nature of men like Sulley, who trained and had depth of quality understanding and predictability.

In 2008, Detroit led the nation in murders per 100,000 residents with 336 homicides; this number topped the statistic of Americans killed in Iraq during the same period of time. See
http://abcnews.go.com/US/story?id=7884362&page=1 and

http://absolutewrite.com/forums/archive/index.php/t-145697.html.

An USA Today Article by Scott Bowles and Paul Overberg June 1999 revealed road rage had accounted for an average 1,500 deaths, 800,000 injuries and a $24 billion medical bill the preceding (http://usatoday30.usatoday.com/news/special/agdrive drive002.htm).

The Detroit News article by Francis X. Donnelly , April 7, 2016, describes the 2008 Scott Johnson ambush on three teenagers at a swimming hole in Michigan's upper peninsula (Detroit News, April 2016).

TEN: TERRORISM

Jerrold S. Maxmen, MD defines reaction formation as exaggerating opposite attitudes to prevent expressions of unacceptable behaviors in *Essential Psychopathology* (New York: Norton & Company, 1986).

Laurence Miller, PhD, who specializes in forensic psychology, discusses terrorism and criminal behavior in his book *Criminal Psychology: Nature, Nurture, Culture* (Charles C Thomas Publisher, LTD: Springfield, 2012).

Autism Spectrum Disorder, according to the *Diagnostic and Statistical Manual of Mental Disorders , Fifth Edition*, identifies structural language disorders as a comorbid feature of autism (Arlington: American Psychiatric Association, 2013).

George Tenet addressed the Great Lakes Homeland Security Conference in Grand Rapids, Michigan in 2002, shortly after he was dismissed by George W. Bush from his position as CIA Director. Mr. Tenet suggested terrorist groups are fueled by disillusioned and undereducated teen males.

BONNIE AND CLYDE

The grit and audacity of Bonnie and Clyde were captured by Virgil Beck in his newspaper article "Bonnie and Clyde Continues Crime Spree in 1934," published in the New York Daily News (1934).

ELEVEN: MURDER AND VIOLENCE RETROSPECTIVE

Tara Culp-Ressler, in her article *Study: Income Inequality Is Tied To Increase In Homicides*, August 1, 2012, points to repeated research citing income inequality as a correlate to increases in homicides. Specifically, when there is unequal distribution of resources homicide numbers increase -

(http://thinkprogress.org/economy/2012/08/01/620401/study-income-inequality-homicides/).

Claire M. Renzetti, with Vivian M. Larkin, reported for the National Online Resource Center on Violence Against Women, in an article entitled *Economic Stress and Domestic Violence,* 2011, the correlation between economic stress and domestic violence (http://www.vawnet.org/applied-research-papers/print-document.php?doc_id=2187).

In research conducted on inmates in an Israeli prison, Ety Elisha, Yael Idisis, Uri Rimor and Moshe Addad engaged in in-depth interviews with men who had killed or attempted to kill their partners. Their article, "Typology of Intimate Partner Homicide: Personal, Interpersonal, and Environmental Characteristics of Men Who Murdered Their Female Intimate Partners" describe hidden needs and insecurities in the perpetrators in the International Journal of Offender Therapy and Comparative Criminology 54, no.4 (August 2010): 494-516.

Ayala Malach Pines provides understanding about how bonding relationships with parents, usually mothers, translates in capacity to form loving relationships later in life in Falling in Love: Why We Choose the Lovers We Choose (New York: Routledge Taylor & Francis Group, 2005).

THE RIPPER

The Dear Boss letter was believed authored by Jack the Ripper and was received by the Central News Agency on September 27, 1888 *(*www.casebook.org/ripper_letters/*).*

TWELVE: SEXUAL MURDER

The FBI reports on serial murder identify and elucidate the crimes committed by Theodore Bundy in Ted Bundy's Campaign of Terror, November 2013 *(*https://www.fbi.gov/news/stories/2013/november/serial-killers-part3-ted-bundys-campaign-of-terror*).*

In her classic biography, The Stranger Beside Me -Ted Bundy: The Classic Case of Serial Murder, Ann Rule paints the backdrop and detailed murders of Ted Bundy (New York: W.W. Norton & Company, 1980).

Editor, Albert Roberts explores the factors contributing to individuals becoming serial murderers, in his book Critical Issues in Crime and Justice. He reports 48% of serial murderers are rejected by parents and the relative commonality of serial murderers being raised by adoptive parents (London: Sage Publications, 2003).

THIRTEEN: SUICIDE

J.M.G. Pollack and L. Pollack, in the 2001 compendium - In Understanding Suicidal Behaviour: The Suicidal Process Approach to Research, Treatment and Prevention – identify distinct cognitive characteristics that lead to suicide (Chichester: Wiley, 2001).

C. Van Heeringen, in "Understanding the Suicidal Brain," reports on in-depth research on what leads individuals to commit suicide and discusses suicidal rates, as correlates with neurological illnesses, cancer and non-responsive epilepsy in the British Journal of Psychiatry, 183 (4) (September 2003): 282-284.

J.H. Meyer, S. McMain and S.H. Kennedy discuss attitudes and how they affect brain receptors and potentially lead to self-harm in "Dysfunctional Attitudes and 5 HT 2 Receptors During Depression and Self-Harm," reported in the American Journal of Psychiatry, 160 (2003): 90-99.

The brave course of Brittany Maynard is elucidated in the article "Terminally Ill 29-Year Old Woman: Why I'm Choosing to Die on My Own Terms" by Nicole Weisensee Egan in a 10/6/2014 article in People Magazine *(*www.people.com/article/Brittany-Maynard-death-with-dignity-compassion-choices*)*.

FOURTEEN: MANIPULATION

Harvey St. Clare, a psychiatrist and assistant professor of psychiatry at the Louisville School of Medicine, is one of the few professionals who wrote about manipulation, in his article "Manipulation" in *Comprehensive Psychiatry*, Vol. 7, no. 4 (August 1966).

FIFTEEN: PSYCHOLOGICAL DISORDERS

The Diagnostic and Statistical Manual of Mental Disorders (Arlington: American Psychiatric Association, 2013), is the diagnostic bible for mental disorders.

Research conducted by Regina Sullivan, PhD. and Elizabeth Norton Lasley is reported in "Fear in Love: Attachment, Abuse, and the Developing Brain" in the *National Institutes of Health Publication*, No. 99-4601 (2010). The researchers discuss fear as a means of survival, but unregulated fear can lead to anxiety and depression.

Steven J. Seay, PhD, discusses the disturbing obsessions individuals experience in his February 2012 article *Hit-and-Run OCD* (http://www.steveseay.com/hit-and-run-ocd/).

In "Psychophysiologic Aspects of Multiple Personality Diorder: A Review" of research by Philip Coon, M.D., aspects of Dissociative Identity Disorder were investigated, which concluded existence of alterations in hand dominance, allergic responses, menstrual irregularities and personality changes. The article was published in *Dissociation 1:1* (March 1988): 47-53.

Dorothy Otnow Lewis and Catherine A Yeager, et.al. conducted research on death row inmates, delving into childhood histories of significant abuse and resulting DID. In "Objective Documentation of Child Abuse and Dissociation in 12 Murderers with Dissociative Identity Disorder," the researchers acquired substantial evidence of savage abuse and survival, published in *Psychiatryonline*, Vol. 154, No. 12 (December 1997): 1703-1710.

Tyrka AR, Waldron I, and Graber JA, Brooks-Gunn J. report on research about causes and histories of those acquiring eating disorders in "Prospective Predictors of the Onset of Anorexic and Bulimic Syndromes" in the *International Journal of Eating Disorders*, 32(3) (2002): 282-290.

Depression often runs comorbidly with anxiety, as reported by the World Health Organization by Norman Sartorius, Behirhan Üstün Yves and Hans-Ulrich Wittchen in "Psychological disorders in primary health care," *The British Journal of Psychiatry*, Vol 168 (Suppl 30), Jul 1996, 38-43.

Hehad Alaedein, PhD and Shaher Hamaideh, PhD, both out of the University of Jordan, studied sense of control and life satisfaction, reported in "Depressive Symptoms and Their Correlates with Locus of Control and Satisfaction with Life Among College Students," in *Europes Journal of Psychology* (4/2009), 71-103.

AUTISM POEM

On the blog *Wrong Planet*, the author of "A Poem I Wrote About Asperger's" is signed Secret Soul, Hummingbird. The poem artistically depicts the struggle and frustration of living in the world of Aspergers.

SIXTEEN: AUTISM

Mary Armsworth and Morgot Holaday discuss the lasting effects of childhood trauma in "The Effects of Psychological Trauma on Children and Adolescents:" *Journal of Counseling and Development: JCD*, 72.1 (September 1993): 49.

Bessel van der Kolk, MD, a world recognized expert in the field of trauma and PTSD, provides deep understanding of the brain changes and neurological systems at play during and following traumatic events. In his best-selling book, *The Body Keeps the Score: Brain, Mind and Body in the Healing of Trauma,* Dr. van der Kolk paints images of how the brain stores, retrieves and copes with trauma (New York: Penguin, Random House, 2015).

Diane L. Williams, PhD, CCC-SLP and Nancy J. Minshew, MD describe language anomalies and neurological pathways of individuals with autism in "How the Brain Thinks in Autism: Implications for Language Intervention," *The ASHA Leader,* Vol. 15 (April 2010): 8-11.

Cynthia M. Schumann, Melissa D. Bauman and David G. Amaral investigate and report on abnormalities of the amygdala in individuals with developmental disorders in "Abnormal Structure or Function of the Amygdala is a Common Component of Neurodevelopmental Disorders," *Neuropsychologia,* 49, no. 4 (2011): 745-759.

Recent studies reveal the amygdale, or the fear center, is initially overactive then shrinks in individuals later diagnosed with autism, reported in "Brain's Fear Center Likely Shrinks in

Autism's Most Severely Socially Impaired," found at http://www.nimh.nih.gov/news/science-news/2006/brains-fear-center-likely-shrinks-in-autisms-most-severely-socially-impaired.shtml.

SEVENTEEN: CONFIDENCE

In an article in the Telegraph, Hannah Furness makes the argument, based on review of literature, that success is more dependent on confidence than talent. See http://www.telegraph.co.uk/news/uknews/9474973/Key-to-career-success-is-confidence-not-talent.html.

Similarly, Mark O'Leary, a noted self-esteem researcher from Wake Forest University, concurs confidence is an important factor in success in an article "Self-Confidence: A Key to Success
(https://secure.gacollege411.org/Home/Article.aspx?level=3XAP2FPAX6J7I3kztATGuYyXAP2BPAXDahIQXAP3DPAXXAP3DPAX&articleId=TKZjBonzsuebU8XAP2BPAXEAiXAP2FPAX11wXAP3DPAXXAP3DPAX).

Albert Bandura, a social psychologist out of Stanford University, underscores the importance of confidence and success in his writings "Self Efficacy," *Encyclopedia of Mental Health,* Vol. 4 (1998): 71-81.

EIGHTEEN: MONEY

A brief history of the evolution of money is unfolded by Andrew Beattie, in a December 2015 article entitled *The History Of Money: From Barter To Banknotes at -*

http://www.investopedia.com/articles/07/roots_of_money.asp#ixzz4Bmqs8Rzx.

Jane Mayer reports in the New Yorker Magazine the political control wealthy special interest business have in the United States, sometimes shaping the political landscape to feed profits in "Covert Operations; the Billionaire Brothers Who are Waging a War Against Obama." See www.newyorker.com/magaxine/2010/08/03.civert-operations.

Forbes Magazine identifies Michael Bloomberg as the 10th wealthiest person in America. Go to http://www.forbes.com/forbes-400/; "The Little Black Book of Billionaire Secrets."

Wikipedia provides a list of the net worth of United States Presidents (https://en.wikipedia.org/wiki/List_of_United_States_Presidents_by_net_worth.)

Stephanie Condon of CBS News reports on the preponderance of millionaires in congress, in *Why is Congress a Millionaires Club?* This March 2012 report discusses the high percentage of millionaires representing the high percentage of middle and lower class constituents. See http://www.cbsnews.com/news/why-is-congress-a-millionaires-club/.

FAMILY GUY

In "Lois Runs for Office," a Season Seven episode of "Family Guy," writers deftly expose, in satirical fashion, the simple-minded vulnerabilities of voters and the dangers associated with an uninformed electorate. Family Guy is a smart, award winning animated series in its fifteenth season. The series airs on Fox Broadcasting Company and was created by Seth MacFarlane.

NINETEEN: LEADERS

Winston Churchill's *My Early Life 1874-1904* is an adeptly written biography by the British leader, laying out his road to adulthood and experiences that brought him to his position as Prime Minister of England during one of the most critical times in history (New York: Simon & Schuster, 1930).

The life and ascension of Franklin Delenor Roosevelt is detailed in the FDR Library website at http://www.fdrlibrary.marist.edu The life and ascension /education/resources/bio_fdr.html.

Robert Dallek captures the life and political verve of John F. Kennedy in his biography *An Unfinished Life: John F Kennedy 1917-1963.* Dallek also wrote an acclaimed book about Lyndon B. Johnson. Dallek is a Boston University History professor (New York: Little, Brown, 2005).

JFK's childhood struggles with illness are depicted in http://www.shmoop.com/john-f-kennedy/childhood-illness-harvard.html. Kennedy, like many successful leaders, overcame difficulty beginning and prevailed over life.

Ileen Bear explores the life of Adolf Hitler in her book *Adolph Hilter: A Biography.* The biography depicts the life of Hitler from childhood to death (New York: Alpha Editions, Penguin,

2016).

Alice Miller explores the aftermath of trauma in children in For *Your Own Good; Hidden Cruelty In Child-Rearing and the Roots of Violence* (New York: MacMillan Publishers, 1980). Miller addresses brain changes and effects as sequela to trauma.

Alison M. Moore reports on sexual anomalies involving popular figures in *Sexual Myths of Modernity: Sado-Masochism, Historical Teleology* (Lanham: Lexington Books, 2015).

Mahatma Gandhi relates his childhood and self-discover in *Gandhi: An Autobiography: The Story of My Experiment with Truth*; Gandhi, one of the most introspective and enlightened leaders of the modern age, elucidates his formative years (Anmedabad: Navajivan Publishing House, 1948).

THE BONOBOS

Anderson Cooper reported on the unlikely discrepancy between two nearly identical tribes of apes, separated by the Congo River, in a *60 Minutes* episode aired December 6, 2015. The Bonobos, unlike their cousins to the north, are non-violent and negotiate disputes through sexual union.

TWENTY-ONE: WORKPLACE

Workplace sexual harassment, as defined by the Department of Labor, suggests advances that are unwelcomed or made through position leverage represent violations of sexual harassment law. Go to https://www.eeoc.gov/laws/types/sexual_harassment.cfm

TWENTY-TWO: CHANGE

Life stressor are identified through use of a stress inventory. The inventory was created by The Stress Organization in Fort Worth, Texas. See http://www.stress.org/holmes-rahe-stress-inventory/.

Spencer Johnson's *Who Moved My Cheese; An Amazing Way to Deal With Change in Your Work and Your Life* was a best-selling book about change and acceptance of change in the late 1990's. Spencer Johnson, MD, wrote a simplistic, yet prolific book about the inevitability of progression (New York: GP Putnam's Sons, 1998).

Thomas Hardy is a pseudonym for a patient who experienced trauma in childhood and reacted violently. While specifics were changed to protect the anonymity of the patient, the core issues were maintained to demonstrate significant points.

WAR AND BENEFITS

Casualties and deaths enumerated through international wars are reported at https://en.wikipedia.org/wiki/List_of_wars_by_death_toll.

TWENTY-THREE: WAR AND POLITICS

A.J. Taylor maps out the disruption of the Hapsburg Empire in The *Hapsburg Monarchy, 1809-1918: A History of the Austrian Empire and Austria-Hungary*, (London: Penguin Books, 2nd Edition, 1964).

Further history of the Hapsburg Monarchy and its ultimate fall can be found at https://en.wikipedia.org/wiki/Habsburg_Monarchy.

Bob Woodward writes about clandestine operations during the Reagan years in *The Secret Wars of the CIA 1981-1987*. Included in the operations was the Iran-Contra Affair, an international and domestic debacle with far-reaching political implications (New York: Simon and Schuster, 1987).

Greg Cashman goes in depth in attempts to understand the reasons and motivations for human conflict in his book *What Causes War?: An Introduction to Theories of International Conflict.* (Lanham: Lexington Books, 1993).

SURVIVAL

Aron Ralson wrote his biography, *Between a Rock and a Hard Place,* following his ordeal in the Utah canyon, in which he was pinned down by a fallen rock and was forced to amputate his arm to survive (New York: Aria Books, 2004).

TWENTY-FOUR: RESOLVE

Michael Inzlicht, Ian McGregor, Jacob B. Hirsh and Kyle Nash discuss brain changes that occur in individuals who maintain unwavering religious conviction in their article "Neural Markers of Religious Conviction," *Psychological Science*; 20 (3): 385 (2009).

The National Center for Complimentary and Integrative Health reports on the benefits of meditation with an article by R.D. Brook, R.J. Appel and M. Rubenfire entitled "Beyond Medications and Diet: Alternative Approaches to Lowering Blood Pressure: a Scientific Statement from the American Heart Association," (*Hypertension 61, no. 6 (2013): 1360-1383.*

John Calhoun authored *"Population density and social pathology,"* a study of population crowding, which affected the emotional health and infant mortality rates of experimental rats (Scientific American 206, no. 3 (1962): 139–148.

TWENTY-FIVE: DETERMINISM

David Hume is foundational to the philosophy of determinism, a position that sometimes conflicts with religious position and, rather, posits foundations of learning and biology as determining factors in behavior. Hume wrote the *Treatise of Human Nature,* first published in 1738, which endures today – edited by David Fate Norton and Mary J. Norton (Oxford: Oxford University Press, 2000).

R.E. Hobart (aka Dickinson Miller) built on Hume's philosophy, but believed there was a component of free-will in decision making. His article "Free Will as Involving

Determination and Inconceivable Without It," was published in *Mind, Vol.* 43, No. 169 (Jan. 1934): 1-27.

John Pickrell authored an article for National Geographic entitled "Humans, Chimps Not as Closely Related as Thought?" Pickerell reports chimpanzees are only 95% identical to human beings. See http://news.nationalgeographic.com/news/2002/09/0924_020924_dnachimp.html.

Tabitha M. Powledge, in a March 2016 article regarding the Genetic Literacy Project, reported humans share 99% of genes with chimpanzees: https://www.geneticliteracyproject.org/2016/03/31/humans-share-99-of-genes-with-chimps-can-dna-explain-differences/.

CONSTELLATIONS

Constellations is a poem written by Loueva Smith and posted May 16, 2015: https://plus.google.com/109559758327965347758/posts/XFjprR2HaZY.